DON'T STEP ON TH

Reflections on leadership, and teamwork

Walter C. Wright

PATERNOSTER

First published in 2005 by Paternoster Press

11 10 09 08 07 06 05   7 6 5 4 3 2 1

Paternoster Press is an imprint of Authentic Media,
9 Holdom Avenue, Bletchley, Milton Keynes, MK1 1QR, UK
and
129 Mobilization Drive, Waynesboro, GA 30830–4575, USA
www.authenticmedia.co.uk/paternoster

British Library Cataloguing in Publication Data
A catalogue record for this book is available from the British Library

ISBN 1-84227-359-0

Cover Design by Paul Lewis
Typeset by Saxon Graphics Ltd, Derby
Print Management by Adare Carwin
Printed and Bound in the US by Dickinson Press

To the rope team
Three decades of climbing
Thirty years of relationships

Donald Bosch
Richard Butman
Donald Dwyer
Newton Malony
Steven Sittig
Brent Stenberg

Contents

              *Teams allow humor to keep things in
              perspective*

9.   **Base camp**   115
              Teams embrace the whole person and family

10.   **Trails and summits**   128
              Teams share something beyond themselves

              Conclusion: On the summit   142
              Team success is measured by legacy

              Notes   148

Preface

What does it mean to tie yourself to another person – to link your success or failure to another person's passions, fears, strengths, and weaknesses? That is what leadership is all about. Leadership is a relationship between two persons in which one person seeks to influence the vision, values, attitudes, or behaviors of the other. Leadership requires followers – someone who chooses to be influenced. Leaders cannot lead unless followers choose to follow. Like it or not, we are tied together. We are a team; we need each other. It is a relationship. And in every relationship both persons influence and are influenced by each other. Sometimes we exercise leadership; sometimes we follow. Leadership connects us.

For thirty years I have found myself in leadership positions – supervisor, middle manager and finally twelve years as president at Regent College, a graduate school affiliated with the University of British Columbia. In 2000 I resigned from the college to continue the legacy of my mentor Max De Pree at the De Pree Leadership Center in Pasadena, California. For the past five years I have been teaching, mentoring and coaching leaders in non-profit organizations and for-profit companies. The more time I spend thinking about leadership, the more convinced I become that we all lead and we all follow as we move together toward shared objectives. There are few settings today where the isolated individual rides alone. We band together; we organize, network and collaborate to accomplish the things we care about. We work in pairs, groups, departments, companies, associations, and networks. Increasingly, small groups of people rather than individuals are becoming the basic molecules of our organizational systems.[1] Our success is linked to the competence and commitment of those around us. We are in it together.

Because I believe leadership is fundamentally a relationship of influence, I have tried to exercise leadership in my various roles with a relational team approach. I believe it is an effective way to release the talent and potential in people – to allow them to lead out of their strengths and competencies. Organizations are not collections of individuals serving a leader. Rather, the leader exists to serve a team of people who *work together* to accomplish the mission that forms the organization or company. Leaders serve teams. Leadership exists within teams.

I think people work better in teams. A team is a particular way of working together. It is more than a work group, more than a collection of people assigned to a project. A team draws power from the relationships between its members to increase its capacity beyond the collective abilities of the members. Teams have life, energy, and momentum. They can be a productive force for companies and organizations if they are encouraged, nurtured, and celebrated. Teams are people tied together – interdependent relationships pursuing a common purpose.

For me, mountain climbing is a powerful metaphor for this kind of teamwork. Over the past thirty years, alongside of my leadership responsibilities, I have belonged to a group of men who climb mountains together, explore the wilderness, and canoe white-water rivers. The climbing rope provides a powerful image of the relational connection between members that ties them into a team – that links each person's success and failure to the passions, fears, strengths, and weakness of the others. Climbers tied into a rope significantly enhance their safety and success; they also increase their risk. Whatever we do, we do together.

The rope that ties the climbing team together is the subject of this book. This is the story of a journey – thirty years of sharing trail and life with six other men, all of whom are leaders in their professional lives. It is a journey I invite you to take with us in these pages. As I reflect on why our rope team has thrived for the past three decades, ten principles for effective rope teams emerge that I believe are transferable to the world of work life and corporate leadership. If more roped-up teams were developed within our organizational settings, I believe we would produce more capable leaders and attain more summit objectives along the trails we choose to share. I invite you as you read to tie into our rope and learn with us about leadership and teamwork.

Walter C. Wright
Pasadena, California
January 2005

Introduction

Ten truths about relational teams that I learned climbing mountains
with friends

The beginning

It was a cool November day as we hiked into the San Gabriel
Mountains for a weekend backpacking trip. This was our first
trip together, a collection of individuals who did not know one
another well, brought together by our common love of wilderness. We were filled with confidence and enthusiasm, but didn't
know what we were doing!

We hiked in jeans and cotton shirts. We had rain ponchos in
case the weather turned bad. Some of us had hiking boots; some
wore tennis shoes. We carried hatchets and knives. Our tents
were inexpensive single-wall summer pup tents designed to keep
off the dew. Our sleeping bags were heavy but would keep us
warm down to 40 degrees. What we lacked in gear we made up
for in food. We carried steaks for dinner, bacon and eggs for
breakfast, and cake for dessert. We were prepared for adventure
and camaraderie. We were not prepared for reality: it snowed!

Flimsy tents collapsed with the first gust of wet snow. Sleeping
bags were warm if we got in wearing all of the clothing we had
carried. Tennis shoes and unsealed boots soaked up water and
froze. Rain ponchos seemed like a good idea until winds blew
them around making it easy for rain and snow to reach our
clothing. And, of course, cotton shirts and jeans get wet very fast

and wick off body heat even faster. Fingers were numb. Toes entered the first stage of frostbite. Bodies hovered around hypothermia. We were cold.

Fortunately we had the hatchets. We used them to chop up the steaks that had frozen solid so we could boil the meat for dinner! The eggs of course were also frozen along with the rest of our food, so everything had to be thawed out inside our clothing using our rapidly dissipating body heat. This was not really fun.

Needless to say, the trip was memorable if not enjoyable. And it started us on a journey that has shaped our lives and our leadership. Realizing how foolish we had been to walk into the wilderness so ignorant and unprepared, five of us signed up for the Sierra Club's Basic Mountaineering Training Course. Together we learned the skills to travel the wilderness with competence and humility. And we learned how to depend upon one another in unfamiliar territory and difficult climbs. When we completed the six-month course we decided to "rope up," literally and figuratively, and began a thirty-year journey walking together in the mountains, in life and in leadership.

The team

At the beginning we were all students, faculty, or administrators at a graduate school in Southern California. We ranged in age from twenty-three to forty-three, with vocational interests in education, business, psychology, and ministry. Some were married; some were not. All of us saw life as an exciting trail into new wilderness, with summits to climb and new horizons to seek. We had in common geographic location, academic environment, completion of the Basic Mountaineering Training Course, and a love of the mountains. That was enough to launch the journey. Starting with that humbling November backpacking trip, we initiated a monthly trip into the California Sierra Nevada Mountains. From 1975 to 1981 we spent a three-day weekend each month in the Sierras and only missed five months in six years. It was a high priority in our lives. We were not professionals; we did it for fun. But we practiced our considerably improved skills, learned to trust one another completely, and continued to stretch ourselves with longer treks, higher mountains, and the occasional white-water canoe trip. We climbed many of the highest peaks in the Sierras, spent five days hiking across a southern pass in the range one summer, and cross-country skied over a northern pass into Yosemite Valley during nine very cold days in February. Probably our most technical challenge was a five-day ascent and traverse of Mt. Rainier in Washington, with a wonderful night sleeping beside the volcano crater. Over these three decades we have become a close-knit, smoothly functioning, effective team.

In the fall of 2004, we went back to Mt. Rainier twenty-five years after our ascent. This time, instead of climbing over it, we walked around it, backpacking the 94-mile Wonderland Trail, remembering our climb, and reminiscing about thirty years of shared life and leadership. And we reflected on the gift this journey has been to all of us. We live all over the country now. Don Bosch is a clinical psychologist and analyst in Pasadena; Rich Butman is a professor of psychology in Wheaton; Don Dwyer is a businessman in Los Angeles; Newt Malony recently retired to Claremont as a Methodist minister and professor of psychology; Steve Sittig teaches high school science in Claremont; Brent Stenberg directs a psychological center in Memphis; and I direct a leadership center in Pasadena. The membership of this small group of men has changed little over the past thirty years. Four of us participated in the first November trip and the Sierra Club course. Brent, Steve, and Dwyer[2] joined the group a little later but have stayed active over the years. Others joined the team and dropped off – by their choice or ours. But that is part of the story of how teams work together.

As our lives unfolded, degrees were earned, careers chosen, spouses married, children born, jobs changed, and we scattered across North America. The monthly trips decreased to four a year beginning with year seven, then dropped to two per year as family and work commitments began to compete with our passion for wilderness and our relational commitments to one another. However, now, thirty years from that first trip, three of us meet for lunch weekly, several gather for an annual winter trip in the California Sierras, and every fall the full group gathers to enjoy what has become the anniversary trip of that first

excursion into wilderness reality. We continue these trips and
honor these commitments because we all still love the mountains
and find perspective in the wilderness. But more than that, we
know that we have found something unique: six other men with
whom we have shared the ups and downs, the summits,
successes, failures, and valleys of our lives. These are men who
know us completely and still like us! Research reminds us, of
course, that the primary predictors of successful life development are quality relationships with peers, teachers, and mentors
with whom we can learn and immersion experiences in which we
have opportunity to face and manage challenges.[3] Perhaps that is
the reason each one of us chooses to tie into the rope that binds
us together as a team, literally on the mountain glacier, but figuratively on the journey of life.

The trail

In this book I want to reflect on that journey, remembering some
of our experiences and identifying some of the truths that we
have learned about life and leadership and the connections of
relational teams. We are a team of leaders. All of us have leadership responsibilities in other parts of our lives, yet we choose to
tie our fate together when we enter the wilderness. Tying into a
rope team is about shared vision, shared leadership – following
as much as leading – caring for one another, and caring about the
rope that keeps us together. As we have reflected on our times
together, each of us has found illustrations to take back to our
own leadership roles, teaching, and mentoring. This book is a
pooling of this wisdom, a collection of stories as remembered by
the group and the learning that we have taken from it. This is a
team project. Later in the book I will talk about the choosing of
leaders for each team objective. I am the team leader for this
project. I undertake it with the encouragement of those to whom
I am roped and the active participation of the two Dons, with
whom I have lunch weekly.

Chapter 1 explores basic definitions about leadership and
teams. We believe that leadership is always a relationship, a relationship of influence in which one person seeks to influence the

vision, values, attitudes, or behaviors of another. Everyone exercises leadership some of the time. We will look at the rope as a symbol of the interdependent nature of the leadership relationship. Leader and follower are roped together. It is an interdependent relationship. Their successes and failures are linked as they move toward the objective together.

The rope defines the team. Chapter 2 explores the meaning of team, looking at diversity and community – to whom am I tied? If our success is interdependent with those on our rope, it is very important that we know who is tied on. This raises questions of team membership, compatibility, temperament, skill, shared values, risk tolerance, and issues of exclusion and inclusion.

Chapter 3 looks at responsibility and accountability. When we tie into a rope team we must accept responsibility for ourselves, for the group, for the relationships among other members, for safety and for shared objectives. Every member of the team is responsible for the health and welfare of the team, and every member is accountable for their personal contribution to that health and welfare.

The rope also powerfully illustrates the shared leadership of teams. One person is given responsibility to lead on each climb. But leadership is more about facilitating the group's decision processes than giving direction. Chapter 4 looks at how decisions are made in a team setting. It faces the question of conflict. What happens when someone steps on the rope on a high glacier? What is the risk to relationship? What happens when someone does not take responsibility for his assignment? What happens when someone does not follow the agreed upon instructions?

Chapter 5 raises the issue of safety and vulnerability in leadership and on teams. When a climber begins a risky pitch, the climber calls "on belay" to ensure that someone on the other end of the rope is ready to hold the climber secure until the difficult section is passed. Leadership is about creating a safe environment in which others can risk growth. Leadership is about trust and confidentiality. Climbing a mountain, like living a life, happens best with encouragement not judgment. Leadership teams mentor one another and encourage leadership development. "What is said on the trail stays on the trail."

Team building is about community building. Chapter 6 examines the social side of the team – its accumulating history and experienced community. Community is about belonging, about contributing, and about benefiting. The campfire has traditionally been a place where wisdom is exchanged, where the defining stories are told.[4] While the campfire is no longer advised in most wilderness areas, the act of gathering around the meal still primes conversation and nurtures community. Meals are times when we stop the hard work and talk about things that matter. This is important in the mountains; it is important in life.

The stories that are retold around the meals, on the trail, and in the car are foundational to the creation of group culture. When I am standing on the edge of a high glacier crevasse it requires patience and trust to wait for someone on the rope team to take another picture. But these "photo opportunities" are recording the shared history that creates and reinforces the culture of the team. Chapter 7 looks at the role of leadership in the formation of culture and the role of culture in shaping the team.

Humor is the focus of Chapter 8. It is a vital element in community building. In no other context of life have I laughed as hard as we do in the wilderness. The immediacy of rope, relationships, and summit provide the luxury of single-issue focus, something we lose too easily in the clamor of life. Risk and survival keep things in perspective in the mountains. Humor keeps leadership and life in perspective.

Chapter 9 recognizes that each person on the team is one face of a much larger network of relationships. We learned early on that the support of family was important to the success of the team. If we were going to go out into the wilderness every month, we needed spouses and children who believed in what we were doing and encouraged us. Conversely, knowing that every person on the rope team was also roped to a family made us take everyone very seriously. Leadership and teams touch the family and extended relationships of the persons to whom we are roped. And strong teams care about what their members care about.

Chapter 10 looks at trails and summits. Leadership is not an end in itself. It is a secondary, supportive responsibility serving the mission – the trail chosen, the summits climbed – and the people to whom you are roped. Leadership is always about results *and* relationships. The shared leadership of teams points the direction and keeps everyone energized for the summit. Effective teams have something in common that transcends the individual. Leadership keeps the focus on what is important and why. It contextualizes every person's contribution in light of the shared objective. And of course a discussion of summits requires us to clarify our definition of success. What is our measure of success? Leadership measures success by legacy. What kind of legacy are we leaving?

Don't step on the rope!

We will explore all of the themes above on our journey through this book, but the element that ties it all together is the rope. The rope is a beautiful image of relationships and thus a powerful metaphor for leadership and the interdependent connections of teams. In leadership and on teams *we are tied to one another*. It's that basic. Leadership is about the relationship of influence that connects two people. Teams are groups of people who have chosen to tie into a common rope. The rope defines the team and leadership moves up and down the rope as needed because everyone on the rope is leader and follower. The rope is that fragile and critical connection tying a team together.

The title of this book comes from our climb of Mt. Rainier. For years I had spent vacations hiking and camping with my family at Mt. Rainier National Park. On a clear day the mountain looms large on the horizon, a dominant presence in the park. Early on I knew I wanted to climb this mountain. So in 1973 I signed on with Rainier Mountaineering guide service for one of their climbs. Over three days, we were instructed in the use of rope and ice axe and placed on teams for a quick ascent to the summit and back. This was my first significant mountain climb and I was awed by the scale of the glaciers and crevasses and inspired by the 360-degree view from the summit. The guide service does this daily, however, so we were rushed up and down the easiest approach to the mountain in two days. This left me wanting more.

It was not hard to convince my friends that we should plan a trip to Mt. Rainier that stretched us and allowed us to experience the full beauty and grandeur of the mountain. We looked up a colleague, John Thompson, a backcountry ranger at Mt. Rainier and asked him to lead us on a climb that traversed the mountain. John had a route in mind he had never taken – up the southwest side of the mountain and down the northeast. At the time we did not realize that this was probably more stretch than we had in mind. Over five days in August 1979 we climbed the magnificent mountain, enjoying a spectacular sunset as we camped on the 14,410-foot summit.

The climb was much harder than anything we had done to date. While our gear was correct and up to date, our packs were heavy and the days were long. On one particularly difficult day we had been climbing for 16 hours. We were tired, and impatient to reach the place where we would camp. As we moved sluggishly up the mountain, the rope between Don and me became slack, dragging along the ground. Tired and not really paying attention, I stepped on the rope as I walked. This produced a sharp and angry response from Don: "Don't step on the rope!" He was right, of course. The rope is the connection between us. There needs to be just enough slack that both climbers can move at their own pace. If the rope is too tight one of the climbers may be pulled off balance. But if there is too much slack the following climber can step on the rope. When that happens, two things can result. First, when I stepped on the rope it stopped the rope quickly, catching Don in mid-step and nearly pulling him over backwards. We were all too tired for this and I deserved his angry retort. But more serious is the potential damage to the rope. When climbers rope up to ascend a mountain glacier they take rope, ice axe, and crampons. Crampons are pointed metal spikes that strap to the bottom of the boot to grip the ice and snow as we climb. The edges are sharp and can easily cut a rope if stepped on. By carelessly climbing along focused on my own tiredness and stepping on the rope, I not only pulled Don off balance, but I risked damage to the rope that connected us, the rope with which we would hold each other secure if we fell. I was tired and thinking about dinner. I should have been thinking about the connection – the lifeline – that we all depended upon. His shout was timely and important: "Don't step on the rope!"

This is the image that runs throughout this book. The rope is the relationship between leader and follower. It is the connection that sustains the interdependence among team members. It cannot be ignored or taken for granted. This is a book about teams – about leaders and followers who rope themselves together to accomplish something greater than they can achieve alone. It is a book about relationships – the intimate connections that separate a team from a group of people. Effective leaders, followers, and team members work to protect and care for the rope – the relationships that make their journey possible. When the rope is cut the climb is in danger.

> Relationships – the intimate connections that separate a team from a group of people

This truth is illustrated poignantly in the book by Joe Simpson, *Touching the Void.*[5] This incredible true story – a legend in the world of mountaineers – was recently made into a powerful docu-drama, visually engaging the viewer in the experiences of Joe Simpson and Simon Yates when they climbed Peru's 21,000-foot Siula Grande in 1985. Simpson and Yates roped together to climb the daunting west wall of the mountain, a route never climbed before or since their attempt. They understood the significance of tying their fate to one another when they roped up. As Simpson said: "The fact that you are tied to your partner means that you put an immense amount of trust in someone else's skill and ability."[6] Tying into a rope team is an issue of personal choice and personal risk. Your future is now connected to the strengths and weaknesses, the vision and values, the skills and abilities of another. And others are tied to you. If one person on a rope team falls, the rest of the team is at risk. Simpson and Yates learned that the hard way.

Climbing for three days on near vertical ice, sleeping through a storm in a snow cave and cutting through deep powdery cornices, they reached the summit exhausted. Their objective achieved, they looked for an easier way back down to their base camp. That proved harder than they expected. With visibility limited by a whiteout storm, they lost their way, fell through an enormous cornice and had to climb back up to the ridge. That night they used the last of their fuel and knew they had to descend the next day. On the descent Simpson fell and broke his leg. Because they were roped, Yates was able to hold him secure while they considered their options. With a badly broken leg there would be no more climbing for Simpson. Yates dug out a solid seat in the snow, tied two ropes together and running them through a descending karabiner carefully let Simpson down a rope length at a time. When the knot connecting the ropes reached the karabiner, Simpson would find a secure position and signal Yates who would unclip the rope, feed the second rope through the karabiner and lower Simpson another length. When Simpson was secure, Yates would climb down to his position and they would do it again. They repeated this process over and over, slowly lowering Simpson down the glacier. But suddenly Simpson fell through a cornice of snow and found himself dangling over an ice cliff, literally at the end of his rope. He could not climb up. He could not shout loud enough to be heard by Yates over the storm. About 80 feet below him was a huge crevasse disappearing deep in the glacier ice. He was trapped. The only thing that prevented his fall and probably death was the rope. He was still tied to Simon Yates.

Up the mountain, however, Yates was in trouble. The seat he cut in the ice was slipping. The knot in the rope had reached the karabiner, jamming it, and the full weight of Simpson's body was pulling him off the mountain. He had no way to know what had happened to his friend. Until Simpson found secure footing to allow slack in the rope, Yates could not move. And Simpson had no place for footing. For 90 minutes Yates sat there holding his friend by the rope, freezing and slowly eroding the security of his seat, while Simpson hung from the rope, freezing and unable to do anything to better their situation. With no other options before them, Yates did the unthinkable ... he cut the rope, knowing this meant his friend was dead. With deep grief and guilt, he slowly made his way down the glacier and back to the base camp exhausted, fingers black with frostbite, physically and emotionally battered. To save his own life he had severed the rope, the relational lifeline to his friend – an act that has been widely critiqued by mountaineering colleagues over the years. The case is extreme, but the illustration is clear. *When you*

*choose to tie into someone's rope, you acknowledge your depend-
ence upon their ability, their decisions, and their actions.* Yates'
life was forever altered because his rope partner fell. In ways
hard to believe, Simpson's destiny was determined by the decision of his partner to cut the rope. The rope – the relationship –
is the lifeline of leadership. It is the bloodstream of a team. It
must be protected and nurtured.

The karabiner: a personal choice

Simpson and Yates tied into the rope with karabiners. This
unique piece of mountain climbing equipment is also pregnant
with image. A karabiner is a three-inch oval shaped metal clip
with which a person ties their personal body harness to the rope.
It is a decision to clip into a rope team, a decision that connects
your strengths and weaknesses with every other person who has
clipped into the rope. For me the karabiner provides an image of
personal choice. We choose to join the team. We choose to
follow a leader. Leadership and team participation are always a
choice. Leadership is always about a choice to follow. There is no
leadership until someone chooses to follow. Teams are always
about choice. A group of people is not a team. The team does not
exist until individuals have chosen to cast their lot with the
others. It is always about choice. Simpson and Yates chose to
rope up to climb Siula Grande. They chose to link their fates to
one another. Every relationship of leadership is an expression of
choice. Every effective team is the result of multiple choices.
Choice is an act of interdependence, a statement of faith, a
commitment of trust.

Joe Simpson and Simon Yates chose to tie into a rope together.
They knew that they were now dependent on each other's decisions and actions. Yates chose to cut the rope. And almost everyone criticized his decision to sever his connection with his
injured partner ... everyone except Joe Simpson. Joe Simpson
lived to tell this story. When the rope was cut he fell 150 feet
into the crevasse landing on a small snow ledge, surprised to still
be alive. Believing that Yates had fallen as well, he pulled on the
rope seeking to take up the slack and reconnect with his partner.

When the end of the rope reached his hand he knew that it had been cut. In desperation he climbed painfully down to a fragile snow bridge where, to his amazement, he saw sunlight and a hole leading to the surface of the glacier. Slowly he made his way up to the hole and out onto the glacier. Over the next three days he crawled, dragging his broken leg, around a maze of crevasses, crossing miles of glacier and mountain rock. With no food or water he lost a third of his body weight. But he crawled into base camp to the shock and astonishment of Yates. The book and the movie capture well the high drama and emotional tension of this story from the choice to rope up together to reflection on the cost of decisions made. Roping up to another can be a life-changing choice.

Leadership is a relationship grounded on choice. We choose to tie together to accomplish a specific objective. Teams are formed out of shared vision and personal choice. In the next chapter we will look at these relationships and why people make these choices.

Chapter 1

The rope

Teams are formed by interdependent relationships

Mt. Rainier

We huddled together, anxiously staring at a world of glaciated ice, sheer rock walls and plunging crevasses, wondering how we would find a trail through that maze. Fear raced around in our minds.

The ascent had stretched our skills and enlarged our experience as we followed our guide up the glacier, around crevasses, over snow bridges and up deep chutes. With map and compass and John's knowledge of the mountain, we were finding our way as we went. There are no trails on high glaciers where routes change daily as cracks appear and crevasses open. We studied the map, we studied the mountain, and we talked. Then, deferring to John's experience, we followed his lead as he cautiously chose a way forward. After a long morning of climbing we found ourselves following footprints. A trail lengthened out before us … sort of. The footprints were a herd of mountain goats seeking a path through the maze of rock, ice, and snow. Clearly not a route chosen by the Forest Service, but a way forward that could be followed. Encouraged, we chose to follow the lead of the goats … until we reached the knife-edge. Following the tracks up a very steep slope, we reached a small ridge and stopped – partly because we wanted to rest and partly because we were afraid to keep going. The hoof prints from the ridge traversed 150 yards along a narrow knife-edge to another solid ridge on the other side. The top of the knife-edge was about 18 inches wide, with steeply sloping sides disappearing like endless slides on our right and left. A common thought screamed in all of our minds: "No way! There is no way I am going to walk out onto that slender sliver of snow!" We sat there for a long time talking about choices and collecting our courage. And we knew John was correct when he said we had no option. The mountain goats were right. This was the only way forward through the field of crevasses. Knowing the truth, however, does not make it easier to act.

But we were committed. We were connected by rope and by our vision to summit, and we knew that a decision to go back down would be equally dangerous and enormously disappointing.[7] So we checked our ropes, our knots, our karabiners, and our crampons. One at a time we slowly inched out across the knife-edge, planting our ice axes deeply in the snow in front of us, moving along like old men with walkers. We looked only at the place where we would put our next foot. To look down either side was paralyzing. But there was comfort in being roped to the others. And fear. The comfort came from knowing that if we fell there would be others on the rope to stop our fall. The fear rushed from the realization that if someone else slipped they could pull us off the edge as well. In fact, if someone fell off one side you might need to jump off the other side to protect the rope team. There was not much room for error. Twenty-five years later, we can all remember clearly the fear that felt so consuming at that moment. But carefully we traversed the knife-edge and celebrated the relative security of hard, flat slippery snow.

From the knife-edge the goat trail led up until we found ourselves at the foot of the Tahoma Sickle, a curving chute of snow leading to the summit of Mt. Rainier. Hard work still, but the goal was in sight and we completed the climb and dropped in exhaustion ready for dinner.

And that became a point of conflict. Our group consisted of two rope teams but three cook groups. I was the organizing leader of this trip. Yet as noted above, John, the backcountry ranger, led the rope teams and chose the route. Each cook group also had a leader responsible for the stove, fuel, and distribution of food. When we arrived on the summit, we set up tents in a stiff wind with temperature rapidly dropping and started dinner. Brent, the leader of our cook group, could not get his stove to light despite several attempts. In his exhaustion, he gave up and headed to his tent, foregoing dinner. I couldn't believe it. I was tired, but I was also hungry and I wanted dinner! We had food but no stove with which to cook. Fortunately another cook group loaned us the use of their stove and we ate well before retiring for the night.

Obviously this has become one of the stories in the culture of our team. In the morning we talked about what happened and how we felt, and worked to rebuild the relationships that were strained by exhaustion, stress, and hunger. (Certainly I would not have suffered much by missing a meal, but I was hungry and very conflicted at that time.) Apologies were given, relationships were affirmed, and commitments were made to see that it did not happen again. While the situation was resolved, for several years after that trip I brought the stove. It was with Brent and his son that I completed the 94-mile Wonderland Trail around Mt. Rainier this past fall. And we used his stove. But I wonder how much residue of the past lingers in the fact that I had a backup stove in my pack.

Descending the mountain seemed like a much easier thing to do. It was all downhill. But the literature of mountaineering reminds us that most accidents in climbing occur on the way down. And once again we found our courage tested. The morning was cold, the crown of the summit icy as we looked for the best route to descend. The curve of the dome made it difficult to see over to select the way forward. John led the rope and ventured out on the ice to see over the edge. He called out to Don to hold him on belay. To belay a climber is to anchor the rope in a way that if the climber slips, he cannot fall far because the rope is secure and will hold the climber until he regains his footing. Usually one climber sitting in a secure seat ideally anchored to a rock or ice axe buried deep in the snow provides a belay. Standing on the ice, however, requires an ice axe or boot belay where the rope is wrapped about the ice axe embedded deeply or, in emergencies, wrapped around a boot whose crampons have been stomped into the ice. When John asked for a belay, Don and I were standing on ice. Neither ice axe nor crampons would bite into the frozen surface. We were standing on top of a giant marble. Don wrapped the rope around his boot, praying that John would not slip. I scratched my ice axe into the hard surface praying that John and Don would not slip. This is one of the few times I remember praying: "God, get me down from here and I promise I'll never do it again!" God kept his end of the bargain. Later John was quite disturbed to hear how precarious his belay had been. John was leading, but he was totally dependent upon the rest of the rope team for his safety and success. Throughout this trip the rope increased both our safety and our risk. It made us a team. By tying into the rope we created a team of interconnected relationships marked by shared fear, shared risk, and shared accomplishment – relationships that weathered conflict. The rope revealed the interdependent relationships between leaders and followers that form the heart of a team.

What is a team?

Jon Katzenbach and Douglas Smith define a team as "a small number of people with complementary skills, who are committed to a common purpose, performance goals, and approach for which they hold themselves mutually accountable."[8] A true team is more than a collection of individuals.

> A team is a new entity in itself, formed out of the relationships among persons committed to a common cause who choose to work together, subordinating their personal agendas to the achievement of team results.

A rope team easily meets this definition. Rope teams can be as small as two persons or as large as five. Too few people on the rope increase the exposure of each climber who has further to fall before slack is pulled tight. Too many people on the rope crowd each climber, not allowing sufficient space and therefore time in which to establish a secure belay. Every team must determine the optimal size and mix that will enable it to achieve its objective.

We will look at team membership and team dynamics in later chapters. This chapter is focused on the rope – the relationships that tie the team together. The rope represents the connections within a social network – the link that binds two or more people together. The rope is not about any single person. It is a relational entity that has meaning only when all of the persons it connects are considered. The rope defines the team; it is about relationships; it connects the members.[9] Several elements important to our definition of a team emerge when we reflect on these connections:

Characteristics of effective teams
shared vision
shared values
delegated results
nurtured relationships
mutual trust
encouraged growth
celebrated achievement
distributed leadership
lavish communication
prized community

A team pursues a shared vision or objective

By definition a team has an objective. People come together to accomplish something important to each person, something they know they can achieve better together than alone. The relationships that bind the team are grounded on the shared vision, the purpose or objective that gathers everyone's focus. Every member of the team is there because he or she wants to achieve the mission that defines the team. Team membership starts with shared vision.

The group of men with whom I climb mountains originally came together because of our shared love of wilderness. Initially we teamed up because we each sought new experiences in the mountains. We were a collection of people with similar dreams that eventually evolved into a team with shared visions and objectives. We became what Jean Lipman-Blumen and Hal Leavitt call a hot group. "A hot group is a special state of mind. It's not a name for some new kind of team or task force or committee. The hot group state of mind is task-obsessed and full of passion. It is always coupled with a distinctive way of behaving, a style that is intense, sharply focused, and full-bore."[10] Highly effective teams I believe have this kind of focus. We started with shared interests, but soon began to focus on specific objectives: Mt. Whitney, Banner Peak, Mt. Ritter, Temple Crag, Mt. Rainier, and the list goes on. The objective of each trip determined the time frame, equipment, and competence needed and sometimes the mix of who could participate.

The vision of Mt. Rainier defined the team that roped up for that climb. Not every member of our group could take a week off work and fly to Washington. Not every person felt comfortable climbing on glaciers. And we needed a guide. New competence was recruited onto the team to help us achieve that objective. And leadership was reassigned.

> Every team is shaped by the vision that drives it. The rope that binds us together has a purpose, an objective toward which each person is moving. It is the purpose that propels the team and the relationships that keep it together.

A team reinforces shared values

Shared purpose keeps the team focused, but shared values hold it together. Not everyone belongs on every team. Relationships sustain the vitality of a team and those relationships are grounded on shared values. Each person joins the team with a unique personality, personal history, belief system, and attitude toward life, wilderness, relationships, time, space, learning, growth, responsibility, authority, and achievement. We learned early on that the intensity of the shared vision or the desired objective impacted the amount of diversity we could accept in shared values. A walk through the city park can tolerate broad difference in personal beliefs and values. But when I am hanging from the end of a rope, I want to be tied to someone who shares my views about life.

Over the years, certain values have risen to the surface in the culture of our mountaineering group, certain ways of thinking about our time in the wilderness. We do not have fires. We stay on the trail when a trail is provided. We believe in God and we seek to preserve wilderness and relationships. If one person wants to rope up, we all rope up. Each person is responsible to keep the person behind him or her in view. No one gets left behind and no one wanders off alone. What is said on the trail stays on the trail. The appointed leader is responsible and has authority to facilitate decisions and the group decision is final. Everyone participates. We turn back when safety is the issue. When we get to the camp we change our socks.

The shared values of the team determine its success as much as the shared vision. We will not continue to clip onto a rope with people whose decisions we distrust or whose agendas differ from our own. Shared values also mean that we confront one another when we deviate from those values. Shared values allowed Don to confront my careless treatment of the rope. And shared values kept a cold stove from separating Brent and me. Shared values are the roots of community. One such shared value is shared leadership.

A team distributes leadership

Leadership is a relationship of influence. When leadership is being exercised, one person is seeking to influence the vision, values, attitudes, or behaviors of another.[11] Leadership is not about position; it is not about person. Leadership is always a relationship between a leader and a follower – a relationship in which both persons lead and both follow. Both participants in a relationship of leadership exercise leadership, both seek to influence the other. Everyone leads at one time or another as each person seeks to influence the vision, values, beliefs or behaviors of those around him or her. However in many ways followers finally determine the presence of leadership. Only when others choose to follow have we successfully influenced their vision, values, attitude or behavior.

Leadership is an act of service to the team. Every team needs a leader. The leader accepts responsibility to influence the team toward the achievement of its objective and the care of its members. The story that comes to my mind whenever I imagine a team without a leader is the poignant story of *Nanda Devi* told by John Roskelly.[12] In 1976, a team of climbers from the United States was organized to climb 25,645-foot Nanda Devi in the Indian Himalaya Mountains. The trip was arranged at the initiative of Nanda Devi Unsoeld, a young climber named after the mountain. A team of highly skilled climbers was assembled, selected because of friendships and extended relationship links. Because they were all friends and because they were all experienced climbers no one person was designated as the expedition leader. Senior climbers shared the leadership, carefully deferring to one another in recognition of the community of talent and abilities present. The objective of the team was achieved. On September 1, 1976, three climbers reached the summit of Nanda Devi. But the climb is not remembered for that achievement. Rather it is remembered as the climb on which Nanda Devi died. The twenty-two-year-old woman became ill at a high altitude camp. But no one was paying attention to the people on this team. No leader had been given the assignment to see that decisions were made and implemented and no one was nurturing the relationships that bound them together. Shared leadership broke down into disagreement and stalemates; no one told Nanda Devi she could not continue the climb, that she had to go back down and recuperate. Many leaders, no leadership. Nanda Devi died from an unknown illness in High Camp IV, a victim of a leaderless team of gifted people. A competent team is not enough. Every team needs a leader with delegated responsibility to serve the team, to see that the mission is pursued, the people cared for and the decisions made.

Leadership is an act of service to the team, delegated by the team for a specific purpose. Every person may have assigned duties for the team's mission, but at any given time one person needs to be assigned the responsibility to see that the team makes the necessary decisions required by its vision and its values. I think shared leadership is one of the defining characteristics of an effective team. On every trip we take, one member is chosen by the team to be leader for that trip. Different leaders are designated for different objectives. The chosen leader – the one we agree to follow – does not direct our activities or make our decisions. Rather he is responsible to see that decisions are made and delegations are accepted. Shared leadership does not preclude the identification of a leader; it recognizes that leadership changes hands as objectives, circumstances, and competence vary. But someone is always chosen to serve the team as leader. On an effective team I think leadership is one of the critical responsibilities delegated and accepted for a purpose and a time.

On the climb of Mt. Rainier I was the organizing leader. I was responsible to coordinate the logistics and the allocation of gear and food assignments. I was also responsible to find the guide, John Thompson. On the trail, John was the leader and facilitated the decisions that needed to be made as we moved up the mountain. Yet at different times on the trip, various members of the team alternated in lead position on the rope, choosing the route and cutting the trail through the snow. Leadership was passed around as needed when something needed to be done. Everyone had the opportunity to influence the decisions that shaped each day. Everyone exercised leadership, and everyone followed.

> When we are tied onto a rope together we are all followers and leaders. Shared leadership keeps the shared vision and the shared values before the team.

A team nurtures results and relationships

Shared vision and shared values keep the team focused on results *and* relationships. Both are necessary for an effective team. Progress toward the vision, the mission that forms us, is measured by the results we achieve together. The values that unite us are measured by the health of the relationships among members. Both are essential. Without a vision, the group is little more than a social fellowship lacking the passion to ignite a team. Without nurtured relationships, the team is mechanical, sterile and will eventually succumb to entropy.

Shared leadership focuses on shared vision and shared values. Because leadership is shared – owned by every person on the team – membership on a team carries the same two responsibilities. Everyone on the team is responsible for completion of the task and nurture of the people. They are woven together as one. In their classic study, *The Management of Organizational Behavior*, Hersey and Blanchard examine the adaptability of leadership required to influence people to accomplish an outcome. Results and relationship – both must be attended to.[13] Leadership adjusts to be more or less task directive in response to the competence of those being influenced at any given moment. At the same time we provide space or support appropriate to the confidence of those following. Leadership is never static, never fixed. There is not one way to lead. Leadership is dynamic and alive, adjusting itself to the realities of mission and the human limitations of those being led. Leadership is a relationship of influence – it cares about results and relationships. The rope that connects the person designated as leader and those who choose to follow makes the team a single entity. The whole rope team, not just the designated leader, owns the vision and the values – results and relationships. Effective teams continue to reflect on what they accomplish and how well they enjoy community.

A team engenders trust

An effective team focused on results and relationships is powered by trust. Trust is the lifeblood of relationship and thus the fuel of teams. Trust is essential for cohesion and community. It is both given and earned. Through competence and behavior, others earn our trust. But the risk of relationship gives trust in faith. This is the vulnerability of trust. Kouzes and Posner put it well:

> Trust is built when we make ourselves vulnerable to others whose subsequent behavior we can't control. If neither person in a relationship takes the risk of trusting at least a little, the relationship is inhibited by caution and suspicion. If leaders want the higher levels of

performance that come with trust and collaboration, they must demonstrate their trust in others before asking for trust from others. That includes going first in the area of trust; it means a willingness to risk trusting others.[14]

Joining a team requires high trust, since outcomes are dependent upon others. It takes trust to accept the team's definition for our success. And the team exercises trust when it embraces us, since we contribute to the corporate outcome. The importance of trust is graphically displayed in the presence of the mountaineering rope. The relationship is tangible, visible. We are tied to one another. This is high trust. Lee Ellis, a former prisoner of war in Vietnam, outlines several key ingredients for trusting relationships: candid, open sharing of feelings, honesty, integrity and authenticity, transparency, genuine concern about the needs of others, careful non-judgmental listening and empathy, seeking and valuing others' opinions, reaching out to initiate help, and having fun together.[15] In a mountaineering team we deliberately create dependencies in order to build trust and cohesion. Meals are assigned, community gear distributed. If someone forgets to bring a lunch we all go hungry. Trust is foundational for our mountain climbing adventures.

A team encourages growth and achievement

A good team is more than just its corporate presence. It is also a community of people. While individual agendas are subordinated to the group objective, an effective team provides opportunity and encouragement for its members to stretch themselves, to learn and to grow. And it celebrates everyone's achievement. Ideally, teams will provide a setting in which each team member can find in his or her teamwork a good measure of personal learning and fulfillment.[16] Great teams find ways for individual members to contribute and achieve, and harness their accomplishment to the success of the team.

When we first started winter backpacking, we entered the wilderness on snowshoes. We carried cross-country skis, but lacked the competence and confidence to ski in with our heavy winter packs. One fine winter morning, I decided to try. We had walked in on snowshoes, set up camp and then explored the backcountry on skis over the weekend. My confidence in skiing was growing with my increasing competence. The morning we packed up to snowshoe out was beautiful and clear. I thought maybe I was ready to strap on my 50 pound pack and ski down the trail to our waiting car. After all, it is downhill all the way and with deep, soft snow I assumed I could risk falling. Everyone watched as I boldly strapped on my skis and hefted my pack onto my back. And they laughed mercilessly as my skis immediately slipped out from under me and I found myself buried face first in two feet of powder snow, pinned down by a 50 pound pack. Fortunately, someone stopped laughing long enough to dig me out so I could try it again. Eventually I succeeded and celebration replaced (or joined) laughter. My risk and humorous learning launched a new era for all of us. We learned about skins – synthetic or mohair strips that adhere to the bottom of your skis and enable much better control of slippage and even some ability to ski uphill. Now Don's homemade snowshoes hang in a closet and everyone skis with degrees of confidence and competence. Teams that encourage members to grow continue to learn and expand their capacity.

A team communicates well

Good communication is critical to the effectiveness of a team. It is at the heart of relationship. Communicating is the bloodstream of trust. It is important that all members of the team know what is happening with individual members. It is most obvious in the assignment of roles. Who will bring what equipment? Who will provide which meal? Who is responsible for which communal activities? After thirty years of wilderness travel together, we do not spend much time talking about this side of communication. Equipment and food assignments are agreed upon before the trip. Once we are on the trail, almost nothing has to be said. Whatever needs to be done gets done. If some are setting up tents, others will start cooking. We often comment as we sit around in the evening that we don't have to worry about how things will get done. Everyone takes care of their own contribution and everyone is watching out for the group, doing whatever needs to be done when it needs to be done. Much of our communication is non-verbal.

But it is also important for the team to know how its members are feeling. This is significant at two levels. First is the maintenance of interpersonal relationships. The team is a network of relationships. Relationships need nurture and care. And the care of relationships requires honest communication of feeling and appropriate feedback. It was important to our relationship and to team safety that Don let me know how he felt when I stepped on the rope. It was important to our relationship that Brent and I talked about the dinner on Mt. Rainier. When we get tired, we lose some control on our temper and patience. A commitment to healthy relationships expects us to talk about these feelings with one another. But there is a second and potentially deadly reason why communication is critical. When climbing high in the thin mountain air, individuals react differently to altitude. While Brent might be leading forward feeling fine, Don might be experiencing violent pain in his head, Rich might be developing serious stomach problems, Dwyer's back might be hurting, Newt might be running out of breath, Steve might be getting hypothermia, and I might have fluid in my lungs. If we don't talk about these symptoms they could kill us. Waiting too long to correct a symptom at high elevation could result at least in exhaustion and inability to go on, and at worst in death from pulmonary edema (fluid in the lungs) or hypothermia (lowered body temperature). No one knows how we are feeling if we don't tell them. Communicating on a rope team could be a life or death matter. Communicating on any team is a matter of success or failure.

A team prizes community over individual performance

One final element required for the development of an effective team is a commitment to the team. A team prizes its community of relationships as highly as its shared objective. An effective team acknowledges the contribution and growth of individual members, but allows members to find their fulfillment in the accomplishment of the team. Being a team is one of the objectives of the team. It is one of the outcomes that is regularly assessed through internal feedback and discussion. *A good team is not a collection of star achievers. It is the star achiever.* Its success is dependent upon every member's contribution and mutual interdependence. Individuals may contribute outstandingly at one moment in time, but the effective team contributes outstandingly over time and individual contributions are secondary considerations. It is the team accomplishment that is celebrated.

Over the years I have read many of the stories surrounding the climbing of major mountains in the world. Mt. Everest, as the top of the world, dominates the literature. There are many stories of expeditions and climbing teams working hard to put a handful of climbers on the summit. Inevitably, the few who stand on the summit are lauded by the world as the achievers. Yet, often, the leader of the team does not reach the top and the hundreds of Sherpas, porters, cooks, doctors, and yak herders, without whose contribution the expedition would have failed, go unnoticed in the celebration. Jean Lipman-Blumen and Harold Leavitt tell one such story about the first successful climb to the summit of Mt. Everest:

When New Zealander Sir Edmund Hillary's team climbed Everest for the first time in 1953, the whole team agreed not to speak about which individual reached the summit first. The important thing, they decided, was that the team reach the summit. They had, perforce, to travel in single file. No individual could possibly have made it without the team.

Then the journalists and nationalists in the United Kingdom and Nepal got into the act. The Nepalese feted Tenzing Norkay, the Sherpa who guided the group, parading him in a seat of honor atop the royal carriage. The rest of the team rode inside the carriage, not visible to the crowd. A UK newspaper was incensed at such behavior, insisting that Tenzing was only a servant/guide and that Hillary, the *real* leader, was the first to set foot on Everest's summit.

Apparently, as a result of all the bickering about who got there first, the friendship between Hillary and Tenzing began to erode.

Hillary's book seemed to imply that he, Hillary, had hauled Tenzing up the last few meters of the mountain, where he lay "flopping like a great fish." Tenzing's book indicated that he had never forgotten that description and continued to resent it.[17]

Interestingly, while many people know the names of Edmund Hillary and Tenzing Norkay, most people cannot recount the name of the leader of that expedition. John Hunt directed the expedition that put Edmund Hillary and Tenzing Norkay on the summit.[18]

A team is not a collection of individuals. It is an entity in its own right – a living organism formed by the people who comprise it and the relationships among them. While a team is made up of individuals who choose to tie onto the same rope, it is the rope team that reaches the summit and the expedition team that makes it possible. As simplistic as it sounds, *being a team* is one of the most important requirements for effective teams. It is the team accomplishments we want to celebrate.

Relationship: virtual rope

In the next chapter we will look more at the individual members who make up our rope team and reflect on the shared values that shape our community life together. When our lives are tied together, it is important to know who else is on the rope. Throughout this book, the rope will be used as the symbolic representation for the intimate relationships that bind the members of a team to one another. The rope visibly ties us together and forcefully acknowledges our interdependence. However, most of our trips do not require the use of ropes. Most are hiking in wilderness, skiing in back country, or paddling in canoes. Yet on every trip, and in life, we continue to act always as though we were tied together as a team. Effective teams are bound together by virtual ropes. It would be well for us to keep those ropes in mind and to know the people to whom we are tied.

Questions for reflection

- On what teams do you share the intimate interdependence of the rope?

- How does your team develop the relationships that sustain it?

- What is the shared vision that defines your team? Has it been articulated clearly and reviewed with team members recently? Has it changed from when the team was first formed?

- What is so important to your team that they would cut someone off the rope before giving up the value?

- How is leadership shared on your team? How could more participation and involvement in decision-making be encouraged?

- What are the barriers to trust? How can trust be encouraged?

- How has each of the members of your team grown over the past year?

- How is information distributed? How do you process the emotional side of communications? How are conflicts managed?

- Who is the star of your team? To what extent is the team the star?

- How do you reinforce the roped-together nature of your team?

Chapter 2

To whom am I tied?

Teams manage diversity within clearly defined community

Changing socks

"You need to change your socks." That seemingly innocuous suggestion led to one person being excluded from the mountaineering group. It was a beautiful fall afternoon, one of our annual October trips into the California Sierras. Like most October trips, we came prepared for summer and winter. In the fall it is not at all unusual to walk into the mountains in shorts basking in warm sunshine and walk out of the mountains in winter gear finding our way through freshly fallen snow. We know this and we go prepared for weather change. This day was typical. Temperatures during the day were warm and comfortable, but we knew the evening would drop close to freezing at our high elevation. This was the trip that a new member had joined the team. Eager to spend time in the wilderness, he asked if he could participate in our trip. We welcomed his youth and energy. But he didn't listen!

After a full day of hiking we arrived at camp tired and ready for dinner. Before setting up the tents and cook system we immediately stopped and changed our clothes. Over the years, we have learned that regardless how warm we feel when we finish hiking, the clothing we are wearing is wet and will wick the heat rapidly from our bodies. It is very important that everything close to our bodies be replaced by dry clothing, especially the socks. Socks feel warm and comfortable when we stop walking but the difference between wet socks and dry socks at camp is significant for comfort and safety. Socks damp from the perspiration of hiking will leave us cold and shivering, even though we put on heavy parkas and wool caps. It is a small thing, but it makes a big difference. We know this; we have done this for years. The new member, however, did not want to be bothered. He put on a parka and sat down to rest. We suggested strongly that he change his socks. He did not listen. As the evening wore on he began to get chilled, started to shiver, did not feel like eating, and eventually had to go sulking off to his sleeping bag to try to get warm.

The rest of us were concerned. Not only did he put his own life at risk, but also his decisions could impact all of us on the team. If one member does not take responsibility for himself, the rest of us will have to. We could understand that he might not have known the truth of our suggestion, but we could not accept his unwillingness to learn from the combined wisdom of the team. He could be dangerous.

And we knew well the high cost that can result from not being prepared and not listening. The autumn before, we had taken a similar trip in the Sierras to climb Temple Crag. As usual we walked in wearing shorts and tee shirts, but our packs included full winter gear knowing the potential changes of October. When we stopped for lunch along the trail, we were passed by another climbing team heading for one of the Palisades near Temple Crag. Several members of their team were known to some on our team. They too were wearing light summer clothing, but their packs also seemed light. We commented on this, noting the unpredictable weather. They laughed at our worries, assured us that the weekend would stay warm and took the fork to the base of their mountain. We continued our trip, arrived at the foot of Temple Crag, changed into dry clothing, and set up our base camp. The next day we would climb. But we did not. That night it snowed. Everything froze. A pole on Brent's tent snapped in two. We woke up to a morning that promised more storms before nightfall. Perhaps because we go into the mountains so often, we have always had a basic principle: if the weather changes we go out and try again another time. So we talked and decided to leave. As we walked out under threatening skies, we wondered about the other team with their summer clothing. Later we heard that they had not aborted their climb when the weather turned bad, but continued to climb in light summer gear. And the price was high. The leader, a colleague of Don and Newt, died on that trip, frozen on his rope, hanging from the Palisade. The elevation was not that high; the temperature not that extreme, but they were unprepared, they made bad decisions, and they did not listen to advice. No one on our team wants to be roped to a person who does not listen and learn.

Our memory of Temple Crag was too fresh in our minds to be pleased that our newest member did not listen. We watched him carefully over the rest of the trip and winced as we saw a pattern developing. When the trip was over there was some debate among other members of the team whether he should be invited along again. In deference to one member, however, we agreed to allow him to join us for a winter ski trip into the John Muir Wilderness. That was his last trip. When advised about the equipment he would need to bring again he did not listen. The skis that he brought were inadequate for the terrain and his skill level and he could not manage them. He grew frustrated and angry and wanted to be left behind. That, of course, we cannot do. A team stays together. One member traded gear with him to enable him to reach our base camp, but neither was pleased when we arrived. His stubbornness meant that we could not ski over Mammoth Pass as intended, so we dug a snow cave and settled in for the weekend. We still enjoyed being in the wilderness again, but we did not invite him on another trip. It is critical that we know well the people to whom we are roped. There is room for diversity on a rope team but within clearly defined limits. Compatibility limits diversity because compatibility is required for team unity to be maintained. A person unaccountable for his behavior, a person who will not listen and learn, is not someone we choose to have on our team.

A team embraces diversity

In organizational life and in community, diversity is considered strength. The inclusion of diverse skills, abilities, perspectives, and experiences enriches the tapestry formed by the interdependent membership. This is true to an extent in the formation of teams as well. Effective teams draw on the varied expertise and experience of their members. Yet the constant interdependence of persons roped to one another requires a high degree of commonality as well. Shared vision and shared values form a prerequisite foundation for team membership. The bounded nature of a rope team (and most other teams) embraces a limited diversity appropriate to the objective.

> A well-composed team strikes a balance between having members who are too similar to one another on the one hand and too different on the other. Members of an excessively homogeneous group may get along well together but lack the full complement of resources needed to perform well. An excessively heterogeneous group may have a rich diversity of talent and perspective but be unable to use it well because members are too different in how they think and behave. In a balanced group, members have a variety of talents and perspectives, yet are similar enough that they are able to communicate and coordinate with one another competently.[19]

Over time the team develops a shared view of reality that shapes the continuing vision and values of the group. This common view limits the diversity acceptable to the team. However, within these limits there is room for and need of diverse interests, skills, experience, wisdom, energy, and commitment. When we decided to climb Mt. Rainier, we needed an experienced guide to help us choose a route. John joined the team as member and leader. Others have come on and gone off as particular goals were pursued. The core of the team, however, has remained stable. And that too is an important ingredient of an effective team. Research has shown that stable teams perform better. They learn together, from and with one another. Over time they develop a shared commitment to the team as well as deepened relationships with one another.[20]

With a spread of age, physical conditioning, and personal interests in our group, there are differences in pace, skill, and commitment. Some members walk faster than others. Early on we learned that everyone has his or her pace. Long legs, weight, altitude, elevation gain, health, conditioning, and a variety of other variables affect the pace we find comfortable. If we push ourselves faster than our own pace, we will waste our strength. But similarly if we walk slower than our normal pace, we will also burn off our energy. People perform best when they can walk their own pace. Recognizing this, a mountaineering team may be spread out along the trail as each person moves forward at the appropriate pace. The only rule we enforce is that everyone is responsible to know where the person behind him is, whether or not we are on a rope team. That way the slowest member is always in sight and no one can get too far ahead. Pace is acknowledged on each trip. Yet not everyone will participate on every trip. Sickness, health, or physical conditioning may cause a member to sit out a particular climb or join us on the trek to base camp but not make a peak ascent. Sometimes the team adapts its objective to the interested members. Sometimes the objective defines the particular mix that forms the team.

Some members are better at rock climbing or working with an ice axe or canoeing a river. When a member has strength in an area, the team looks to him for leadership and the strong member is expected to assist those with less experience. The strongest climber is usually the lead on a rope team, with the less experienced immediately behind the leader. Teams make adjustments around the strengths and interests of their members. I feel strong when we are hiking or climbing and have no problem taking the lead, but when we put a canoe into a rapidly rushing river my stomach churns. This is Don's world; if I choose to participate I lean heavily on his expertise, even though (or especially because) that dependence has dunked me in the river several times!

There is also intellectual diversity. Members of a team bring their lifetime of experience and learning to the team. New ideas, research, critical issues, controversies experienced or studied, life struggles and joys, theology and faith commitments differ from person to person. When the team works together, they talk together and intellectual capital is expanded as well as competence and confidence in the mountains.

Because we are each unique individuals, there will always be diversity within an effective team. However, I believe that the intense focus and interpersonal relationships which set a team apart from other organizations and communities limit diversity. Diversity on a team is always bounded by the shared vision and values that shape the common view of reality before us.

To whom am I tied?

When we are dangling from the end of a rope, we have a strong vested interest in knowing who's holding the other end. Life and death perspective focuses our attention on the relationships that shape our fate. But we do not have to fall to appreciate who is on our rope. As soon as we clip in, we have created interdependency with everyone on the team. To apply a much-quoted phrase from Max De Pree, we have abandoned ourselves to the strengths and weaknesses of the others.[21] Because our direction, pace and abilities are now shaped by every person on the rope, it is essential we know to whom we are tied.[22]

While the rope makes this truth obvious to mountain climbers, it is equally valid for any team of people seeking to accomplish something together. The people who make up the team bring their strengths and weaknesses to the effort; their personalities, emotions, dreams, and fears; their experiences, competencies, and failures. If we are going to work together it is important to understand why each member is on the team – what they contribute, what they seek to accomplish, and what liabilities they add to the mix. What makes a team effective is not homogeneous similarity, but relational harmony and complementary contributions. It is the synergistic unity that makes a team capable of achieving more than any one of its members could attain alone.

So the mix of members becomes important – the balance between diversity and similarity. Diversity enriches capacity and raises questions of team size and appropriate skills. At the same time, team unity and cohesiveness require a high degree of compatibility, respect, and trust. Since teams are formed to achieve a particular outcome, the destination or objective may define the diversity required, but the relationships comprising the team will be nurtured by respect and trust. Trust is given and earned and contributes to the stability that allows the team to perform effectively over time. Such trust tends to grow best where there are shared values. These shared values shape the team community, but they also cause people to leave when there is no longer an appropriate fit. Each team then has to determine the appropriate answers to some basic questions:

- How much diversity is acceptable?
- How articulate are shared values?
- How well does each member know themselves and the strengths and weaknesses they bring to the team?
- How committed is each member to managing the relationships that determine the effectiveness of the team's work?

The answers will vary from team to team. They may differ for the same team when new objectives are pursued. The critical question for all teams, however, is: *How well do you know the people on your rope?*

Diversity enriches capacity

When we first began to explore the mountains in winter, we carried heavy packs stuffed with warm clothing and cold weather gear. We had learned well from our initial foray into the wilderness and our training with the Sierra Club. We carried four-season tents designed to withstand howling winds, pelting rain, and heavy snow. In fact, we were quite comfortable. Then we invited a new member to join us.

He was a walking advertisement for *Outside* magazine. He was equipped with state-of-the-art mountaineering gear. He was young, strong, and aggressively pushing his limits. He wanted to learn new things, explore new areas, and test his abilities. When he joined the group he added new knowledge to our mix. Together we learned more about advantages and disadvantages of different equipment. And he introduced us to snow caves. We had all read about snow caves, but none of us had tried to build one, let alone sleep in one. The new member wanted to try it. So we spent a day digging a deep cavern into a bank of snow. We tunneled down low for the entrance and then up higher to create a sleeping platform that would accommodate four persons. Crawling through the three foot tunnel we entered a large, completely enclosed domed space, totally dark and protected from wind and snow. While the outside temperature dropped below freezing at night, the inside space stayed a comfortable 30 degrees. But ... it felt claustrophobic. Lying on the floor of the cave with three to five feet of snow over our heads immediately brought to mind images of being buried alive. Anxiety levels increased dramatically. The concept sounded much better than the reality. So we decided to sleep in the tent. The new member, however, needed to test his limits and decided to sleep in the snow cave that night. The rest of us slept lightly, ready to dig him out if everything collapsed.

The snow cave held up well and our newest member had a restless but secure night's sleep. In the morning, we skied across the top of the cave and it still held its shape strongly, so we all decided to test the cave. That was the beginning of a new facet of our winter trips. Since he lived through the night, we decided the rest of us could probably risk an attempt. Over the years, we have occasionally taken the time to dig snow caves, some large enough to hold six men, and spent wonderfully comfortable nights in their womblike embrace. While claustrophobic images still float at the edges of our minds, we have learned to trust the construction and delight in the absolute silence and darkness of the cave. A few candles lighting the space make reading and conversation easy. A new capacity was added to our team. And it took a new member to make that happen.

> Diversity enriches capacity. Each person added to a team brings his or her knowledge, skills, experience, and interests to the group. That is the primary advantage of teams.

Together we have abilities that exceed the capacity of any one of us. Each member adds something to the mix, brings a contribution that strengthens the team's capacity. On Mt. Rainier we needed an experienced guide. When we are negotiating a whitewater rapid I am pleased to have Don's skills in my canoe. When I joined a trek to the Mt. Everest Base camp I was very glad to have a doctor on the team with wisdom about high altitude sickness. When we want to record the beauty of the mountains we visit, we look to Brent's artistry with a camera. Diversity strengthens the team by expanding its experience, its skills, its knowledge, and its spirit.

Each person added to the team brings a unique contribution, which raises the question, *How big should a team be?* I don't think there's a simple answer to this question. Sports teams range from two in tennis to eighteen in Australian rules football. On a mountaineering rope it is clear: team size must range between two and five. It takes at least two to make a team. Two is the minimum for a rope to offer any advantage. If one falls there is another to take up the slack. Five, however, is the maximum for safety. Any more than that and the climbers are too close together to have time to react to a fall before it takes them down as well. On a good rope team, the climbers are far enough apart for others to position themselves and hold a falling person secure until he or she can regain his or her footing. I like the rope analogy. I think an effective team is small enough for every member to know each person on the team – the rope – and be prepared to take up the slack if any one of them stumbles. Richard Hackman experimented with group size in his Harvard classes and concluded, "A team cannot have more than six members. Even a six-person team has fifteen pairs among members, but a seven-person team has twenty-one, and the difference in how well groups of the two sizes operate is noticeable."[23] In the end, the question of size is shaped by the importance of the relationships. Teams are defined by their destination, but their effectiveness is determined through their relationships and their communication.[24] The matter of team size is correlated to the number of persons in which we can invest sufficiently to know them well.

In mountain climbing, small rope teams are often part of larger expeditions. It takes dozens of people to put the supplies in place to ensure that a climbing team can reach the top of a major mountain. Perhaps there is some value in making this distinction for all teams. *A team is a small group of people working together on a common objective, dependent upon one another's contribution, knowing each other's strengths and weaknesses, caring about each other's growth and development, and holding one another mutually accountable.* Anything larger than that is an expedition, an organization.[25]

Compatibility contributes to unity

The ability of a team to work effectively is directly proportionate to the strength of its *relationships*. Teams depend on trust and mutual respect to hold them together.[26] It is this basic compatibility that brings synergy to the task. Teams work *together*. It is this cohesion – this togetherness – that creates the spirit of unity that focuses a team's effectiveness.[27] Some of this comes from compatible personalities, similar temperament, but unity usually requires more than that. Shared vision, shared values, common mission, shared opportunity, commitment, and relational accountability all contribute.[28]

When we head into the mountains, we have a shared objective to which we bring our particular skills, varied experience, and multiple interests. *And we enjoy being with one another.* That is important. We get along; we are comfortable in one another's company. And that relational comfort contributes to making us a team, allowing us to bring our strengths to the task, knowing that others will compensate for our liabilities. This compatibility, this sense of belonging, is critical. Without it, the team is little more than a collection of individuals. A group of gifted individuals is not a team. An effective team requires interdependent members working together. A relational team leans heavily on the relationships that comprise it. Trust and respect are enjoyed, nurtured, and enriched over time.

Stability enhances performance

Relationships are living things and they need to be tended and nurtured as they grow and develop. Over time, trust and respect are cultivated and strengthened. This contributes to the stability of a team, and stability enhances performance. The longer people work together, the better they understand who brings particular strengths in one area or needs to be assisted in another area.

There are many reasons why reasonably stable teams perform better. Members develop familiarity with one another, their collective work, and the work setting, so they are able to settle in and focus on working together rather than waste time and energy getting oriented to new coworkers or circumstances. They develop a shared mental model of the performance situation, one that, with time and experience, is more integrative than the individual models with which they began. They develop a shared pool of knowledge, accessible to all.[29]

As we have watched our mountaineering group evolve over the years, we have noted how much of our work together becomes second nature. We know whom to look to for specific strengths. We anticipate what needs to be done and do it without direction or communication. Thirty years of hiking together creates smooth, almost instinctive working together, whether planning, on the trail, or in camp. It has also shaped the community we have become.

Shared values shape community

The destination defines the team. The class of mountain we intend to climb determines who can clip onto the rope; the force of the rapids selects who will go canoeing; the length of the trip limits who can participate. Competence and contribution are critical to team success. The actual configuration of the team will vary from trip to trip. But the shared values of the members remain constant. It is the shared values that shape the community – the relationships that fuel effective teams. Shared values increase the compatibility and unity and promote the stability that enhances the team's performance over time.

Every organization, every team forms a corporate culture over time. That culture represents the accrued beliefs, assumptions, and values that have interacted over the years and established the "way things are done." As Edgar Schein tells us, the assumptions of the culture are usually hidden and taken for granted, controlling behavior without conscious thought.[30] After thirty years of wilderness travel together, the shared values of our rope team have become part of our culture. We do not need to talk about them.

We assume them. They shape the way we choose to work together. Consequently we are always surprised when someone violates these values and acts in a manner inconsistent with our culture.

The most recent new member was a case in point. His need to test himself continually eventually eliminated him from the group. At first we were challenged by his ambition; it stretched our own learning. However, as time went on, it became clear that his risk tolerance was much higher than the rest of us on the rope team. His desire to push his limits led him to take risks that the rest of us thought unwise. We wanted to enjoy the wilderness; he could not enjoy the trip unless he was at risk. The incompatibility was clear. I'm not sure if we stopped inviting him because he was never satisfied or if he stopped participating because he wanted to find more extreme adventure. He joined our group only for three trips and then went off on his own.

The new member's continuing need for risk was acceptable for an occasional learning experience, but not compatible in our group as a way of being in the wilderness together. He did not remain part of the team. It was not a good long-term fit for him or for the rest of us. *Shared values shape the community partly by excluding some who might participate.*

Another friend joined the team for several trips, but brought a personal desire for independence and solitude that caused him to wander off on his own without telling anyone else. While we enjoyed his company and held most other values in common, it concerned us that we could not always be sure where he was. The rope team places a high value on the group. We can give one another space, acknowledging that Dwyer likes to stay up late alone, that I like to walk in silence on the trail at times, or that Brent needs time to take pictures. But we take responsibility for one another's safety and need to know where everyone is. For that reason we have a cardinal rule – you are always responsible to know where the person behind you is, even when not roped up. The connectedness of the group is important to us. We do not embrace the "anarchy that can come when each member of a group or organization heads off in whatever direction is personally most agreeable."[31] The highest shared value for our team is the community among its members. We care deeply about enjoying the wilderness together. The relationships are important.

Safety is important. We are in this together; we share the same rope. For a team to sustain the community relationships that support its shared mission, high priority must be given to the shared values as perceived by its members.

Self-knowledge is the foundation for leadership and team membership

With the importance placed on community and relationships it is critical that members know themselves – their strengths, weaknesses, values, and fears. We are assets *and* liabilities on the rope and we need to understand both dimensions. The man who would not change his socks was not aware of his limitations and that made him dangerous. I know that I have more energy in the morning and that I am weak when we start a climb in late afternoon. Don knows that altitude affects him more severely than it does the rest of us. On the other hand I get unrealistically euphoric on mountaintops. When most of us climb eagerly into our sleeping bags at 6:30 p.m. on a freezing winter night, Dwyer knows that he can't possibly sleep without staying up longer. I am very uncomfortable in single-person kayaks and lack the competence to steer from the stern of a canoe. Dwyer prefers the control of the kayak and Brent would prefer not to be in either. We all bring strengths and limitations to our participation on the team and it's critical that we understand what they are.

Over the past few years much has been made of emotional intelligence. Daniel Goleman and his colleagues have brought this important component of leadership and team relationships to public recognition. Emotional maturity is more important to leadership, to relationships, to team effectiveness than competence or intelligence.[32] Humans are relational beings. We are governed by emotions as much as thought. The research on emotional intelligence underlines that the foundation for leadership and effective teamwork is self-knowledge – self-awareness. People who are aware of their strengths and weaknesses and how they emotionally respond to events are able to exercise self-control – to manage their words, emotions, and actions in relationships with others.[33] Effective teams will be built with people who know themselves, manage their emotions, and develop their technical and relational skills.[34]

Relationship management is at the heart of team life

If self-awareness and self-control are foundational to relationships and leadership, relationship management is at the heart of team life. Teams are networks of overlapping relationships, and relationships must be managed. If emotional competency rests on self-awareness, it finds expression in relationship management.[35] Building, nurturing, and protecting relationships is essential to the effectiveness of a team. Again, *relational cohesiveness is what sets teams apart from work groups.* It is not sufficient to develop technical competence or recruit star performers. The relationships that knit individual members into the tapestry of a team must be managed – by team leaders and by every member of the team.[36] Relationship management cannot be delegated. It is the responsibility of every member of the team. Relationships are managed by listening, by communicating with empathy, by trust, respect, understanding, and acceptance.

On a wilderness trip we talk. We talk in the car on the way to the trailhead. We talk on the trail. We talk over meals. Between trips we communicate by telephone and email, and three of us have lunch weekly. We talk about our hopes and our dreams, our fears and our anxieties, what we are learning and what we want to learn. And we listen. We listen well enough to hold one another accountable to our vision and our values. We follow up with one another on larger issues of life. We talk about conflict, whether it is stepping on the rope, failing to cook dinner, dumping the canoe, or any of the myriad other ways that people roped together can impact one another. And we create a safe place for exploring ideas and sharpening relationships. As noted above, we have another cardinal value: What is said on the trail stays on the trail. This group of men with whom I have climbed mountains for thirty years knows me well. They know the good and the bad that shapes the person I am becoming. They know who I am and who I want to be. And they like me anyway! Communicating is fundamental. It is about talking, but it is also about listening and then acting on what you have learned with responsibility and accountability. People who are not aware of themselves, who do not listen and learn, who do not value the cohesiveness of the team are liabilities and probably will not continue as members.

We did not invite back the person who would not change his socks. We did not invite back the person who wandered off without warning. And the person who wanted more risk discontinued participation with everyone's understanding. Effective teams manage their diversity within the strong bounds of the shared values that form their community. It is this community – this network of relationships – to which each member belongs and for which each team member has responsibility and accountability.

Questions for reflection

- What is the most important thing in life to you?

- When your life is over, for what do you want to be known?

- What do you contribute uniquely to your team?

- What does each member of the team contribute?

- What values constrain the selection of members for your team?

- What are the core values that articulate how your team works together?

- Write down the names of three persons on your team; write down their spouses' names, the names of their children. Why did they choose to join the team? What is their vision of team success? What dreams and hopes do they have for their life? How well do you know the people on your rope?

- What do you admire most about each person on your team?

- Who have been the long-term 'pillars' of the team? Why?

- What does 'community' mean in your context?

- How do you get feedback on team participation?

- How much face-to-face time do you spend with each member of the team?

Chapter 3

Whose rope is it anyway?

Teams share responsibility and mutual accountability based on trust

Who "owns" the rope? The ambiguity of this question embraces two images on our journey together: the rope to which team members clip themselves to climb a mountain and the relationships that connect each person to the others. The physical rope may belong to one person who contributes it for the trip, but when the rest of us tie in, the rope is owned by all. The virtual rope that connects us relationally is always owned by every member of an effective team. Effective teams hold one another accountable for their individual contributions to team results and relationships and they share responsibility for the health of the team's corporate vision and values. Every person on the team is responsible for team objectives and outcomes and every one is accountable for their personal decisions and behavior. Teams depend upon individual contribution but expect higher commitment to corporate results and relationships.

Teams depend on responsibility and accountability

When we gathered at Saddlebag Lake high in the Sierra Nevada Mountains, we brought the equipment necessary to climb the glacier to the summit of North Peak. Climbing rope, shovel, map and compass, tent, stove, fuel, cook pot, and food belonged to the group gear. Ice axes, crampons, sleeping bags, first aid supplies, and clothing were personal gear. Each piece was necessary, but not everyone needed to bring every item. Everyone needs a sleeping bag, but three people can share a tent. Everyone needs ice axe and crampons, but five people can share a rope. In our case Don and I bought a top quality climbing rope together. We own it; we store it at Don's house, but everyone considers it team gear. If Don forgets his ice axe, he does not climb. If he forgets the rope, no one climbs. Early on, I bought an MSR expedition stove and cook pots to go with it. For years it was expected that I would bring the stove, fuel, and pots as my contribution to team gear. Everyone should have a map and compass, but Don and I always bring them as a contribution to team equipment. My shovel, Dwyer's bear canister, and sometimes Brent's camera are delegated responsibilities contributed to the team. Similarly, food assignments are given: breakfasts, lunches, and dinners are allocated to various members who are expected to choose the menu, do the shopping, provide the meal, and clean up afterward. Tent assignment varies as well. Each of us has purchased one or more tents over the years and who will bring the tent is usually determined by the size of the team, weather conditions, and the degree of weight-consciousness we are protecting. Brent has a three-person summer tent weighing three pounds. Don has a three-person winter tent weighing 11 pounds. The rest of us have something between. Who owns the equipment, however, is not the point. The point is that all members are expected to contribute to the group gear (and share in carrying it) as well as provide their own equipment. One person's failure to bring group gear or personal equipment impacts everyone on the team. The team depends on personal responsibility and accountability.

Team members are responsible for themselves

Every member is accountable to the team for his or her own physical condition, equipment, and competence. If someone buys new boots, we expect them to be broken in before the trip, so that one person's painful feet do not slow the whole group. Each person is expected to monitor his own health because poor physical conditioning impacts everyone on the rope. When we took the 94-mile trek around Mt. Rainier this past fall, Don decided to join the team. Don, however, had recently damaged his knee while rebuilding his house. He limped painfully everywhere he walked. But he wanted to participate and Don is one of the founding members of our team. He bandaged his knee, took pain pills, used trekking poles to balance his weight, and committed himself to the first 35 miles of the trek. He was in pain the entire time, limping along at a slower pace than normal, resting frequently. He was aware that his pain was slowing down the team, causing us to take much longer to walk the 11-mile sections each day arriving later in camp for the night. But we were committed and Don is a stubborn Dutchman! He swallowed his pain and limped along and we were glad to have him. However, when we reflect on that trip, Don recognizes that it was a mistake for him to go. With his injured knee, he did not bring his full strengths to the team. He became a liability. The daily decisions of the team wrapped around Don's condition and the pace he could maintain. Had his knee grown worse, we might have had to scrap the rest of the trip. Team members are responsible for their personal contribution to the group. Accurate self-assessment and honest communication of strengths and weaknesses is everyone's responsibility. When you are part of a team, your contribution impacts everyone else – both your personal condition and competence and the delegated assignments you have accepted.

> When you are part of a team, your contribution impacts everyone else – both your personal condition and competence and the delegated assignments you have accepted

One spring, my family invited a couple to join us for their first wilderness trip. I was the designated leader. I gave them a list of the personal equipment they would need and agreed that I would furnish all of the group gear. We met at the trailhead and entered the mountains for the weekend. It was a great trip … until evening. Only then did the couple realize that they had not packed their sleeping bags – a rather important item for spending the night in the mountains! It was their mistake, but on a team it becomes a group problem. We either figured out a way for everyone to sleep comfortably or we aborted the trip and returned to the comforts of home. In this case, those who sleep warm contributed sleeping bags, we spread extra clothing around, and everyone found a comfortable way to sleep soundly and warmly. It ended up being a good weekend, but perhaps the last time that couple ever camped together. The team depends on team members taking responsibility for themselves as well as for the team.

Teams are comprised of individuals who contribute a particular competence to the shared purpose. The team depends upon this contribution to live out its shared vision and values. Effective teams corporately and individually hold one another accountable for their participation. The condition or health of a member is as important for a work team as it is for a rope team. Teams expect members to bring competence – knowledge, skills, experience, delegated responsibilities – and they need members to continually sharpen that competence and strengthen their contribution. The responsibility for competence and contribution rests completely upon the individual member, but the accountability is to the whole team as members trust one another enough to rope together with mutual dependency.

Team members are accountable to the team

The effectiveness of a team is directly proportional to the quality of each person's contribution to the shared vision and values. Individual actions impact everyone on the rope. It is critical that teams communicate clearly the expectations they have for each member and corporately hold one another accountable to the team effort. When a team member's contribution fails to meet expectations, everyone on the team feels the fallout.

While our mountaineering team has been very diligent about these responsibilities, I have participated in some teams where such responsibility was lacking. Ron was a wonderful man, an adventurer who loved the outdoors and hiked extensively in the mountains of the Northwest and kayaked both river and ocean. Organization, however, was not his strength. I joined one trip on which he was the designated leader, a wilderness trip to explore a deserted island off the coast of Canada. He took responsibility for obtaining a boat, arranging shuttle transportation, and bringing the tent. I brought the stove, fuel, pots, and food. When we arrived at the dock on Vancouver Island from which we would depart by small boat, I noticed a small outboard engine but no oars in the boat. I should have said something then. The slow cruise up the Georgia Straits started out smoothly. It was a beautiful day. However, we were less than a mile off shore when the motor died and nothing we could do would get it started again. That, of course, was the moment everyone realized that we did not have oars. The backup propulsion was one small canoe paddle which enabled us to hold our own against the current but make very little progress toward shore. Fortunately, a sailboat happened by and, to the chagrin of our adventurous leader, towed us back to the dock. On shore, the motor was replaced, we added oars to our inventory and continued across the Straits without further difficulty. We reached the small island and prepared to set up camp with a magnificent view of the sun setting behind Vancouver Island. That was when I saw the tent. It was a huge army surplus canvas tent which under some conditions might have been acceptable ... except that Ron had forgotten the poles and stakes! It turned out he had never set it up before. Improvising wildly, we used branches, driftwood, and stones to secure the tent, praying for calm weather through the weekend. It rained. However, with a few excursions out of the tent to shore up its sides during the night, we managed to keep dry and sleep five in the tent with some degree of comfort. The rest of the trip was uneventful and quite enjoyable. Nothing was damaged but Ron's pride and my blood pressure, but we knew we were fortunate. Bad weather could have left us in miserable conditions on the island and without the passing sailboat who knows how long we would have floated adrift. The team

> Teams depend on personal accountability

depends on individual members' accountability to one another for their delegated responsibilities. If an individual member doesn't deliver his or her contribution to the team, the whole team suffers, the mission is at risk. Every member is responsible for the health, safety, and success of the team.[37]

Open communication reinforces accountability

While each person is responsible for him or herself, the team can play an appropriate role in asking questions of its members as a way of reinforcing expectations. This does not relieve the individual of responsibility. However, because each person on the team cares about everyone else's contribution, relational communication provides some backup redundancy. Our mountaineering group regularly talks through checklists of things for which individuals are responsible to remind one another of our responsibilities and to step in if something needs to be addressed for the sake of the team. Because we all have a high commitment to the safety of the group and the objective of the team, we give one another permission to ask us the questions that ensure that the supportive details as well as the larger mission are kept in focus. We always ask about keys!

Asking questions reinforces expectations

This one we learned the hard way. Brent, Don, and I planned a weekend trip on a 20-mile stretch of trail in Washington's Cascade Range. It was a one-way trail and required a car shuttle. Brent flew in from Tennessee, rented a car and drove to Box Canyon where we would be exiting the mountains. I picked Don up at the airport and drove my car to Box Canyon, picked up Brent and drove around the mountain to our starting trailhead. It was a good plan. By trail it was 20 miles from car to car; by road over 35 miles. We loaded our packs, left our traveling clothes in the trunk of my car and set off on a beautiful hike through fields of Indian paintbrush, blue lupine, and avalanche lilies. The first night was spent in a high meadow with mountain goats grazing on a hillside nearby. On day two we moved deeper into the wilderness, crossing the ridge crest at the 10-mile mark. It was at this point that Brent began to fall back, clearly deep in thought. Respecting his solitude, we walked on, marveling at the valley with over a dozen waterfalls cascading down its sides. However, when Brent caught up with us and opened the conversation with "Guys ..." we knew something was wrong. We stopped so he could look through every pocket and pouch of his pack searching for the keys to the rental car that waited for us at the end of our trip. After a thorough search, we concluded that the keys had been left with his travel clothes securely locked in the trunk of my car back where we started. A small thing, but it required a team decision. We were now half-way through the trip in time and distance. Since we believe strongly that the group stays together, we did not seriously consider sending Brent back for the keys, although I am sure it was suggested a few times. Our choices were to retrace our steps and return to my car over the next two days or continue as planned and hope we could secure a ride from Box Canyon back to the trailhead. Together we decided and chose to finish the trip as planned. Obviously we did get a ride back to the trailhead, but it was not as easy as we had hoped. Three men emerging from the woods, unshaved and unkempt, raise more caution than compassion! No one wanted to give us a ride. For most it was a 70-mile trip out of their way, but even people heading in our direction were afraid to take one of us into their car. After several hours of pleading, begging, and attempting to purchase transportation, I finally obtained a ride from a young special ops Green Beret recently back from the Gulf War. He was not afraid to let me in his car! In hindsight, perhaps I am the one who should have been afraid ... but we needed a ride. As with most of our stories, this one ended well, but never again will we enter the wilderness without every member of the team knowing where the keys are. And Brent may be the first to ask.

Teams talk. They communicate. Because everyone is committed to the outcomes, everyone has the right and the responsibility to question and encourage the other members.[38] We share the rope. We're in this together. If my questions help you perform better, we both gain because the team gains. A small lapse – stepping on the rope, misjudging conditioning, forgetting equipment, or leaving the keys – can impact the whole group. In the mountains it could be fatal. And because we care about the mission that brings us together, we encourage one another to look over our shoulders, to back us up, to ask us the questions that sharpen our ability to contribute to the team. Effective teams are aware of everyone's participation and while they do not do the work for individual members, the team provides encouragement and others are ready to step in when a member needs help.

Team members accept responsibility for the other members of the team

Mt. Ritter is one peak that has eluded us. Three times we have tried to climb this 13,000-foot peak in the Sierra Nevada Mountains. And three times we have been turned back. One of those times was nearly tragic.

Don, Newt, and I were making our second attempt on this summit. After hiking 10 miles in to a base camp, we roped up together and ascended the glacier up the southeast side of the mountain. It was a beautiful day and the climb went well. Along the way, Joe, a solo climber, caught up with us and attached himself to our group for safety. At the top of the glacier, we entered a steep snow chute leading to the summit ridge. It was slow work, step by step up the chute, but we reached the ridge well before lunchtime. The summit was in sight. On the ridge we could scramble up a rock band to the summit, so we untied from our climbing rope and proceeded toward the summit. About that time we noticed a change in the weather. Dark clouds forming on the horizon were moving rapidly in our direction. A storm was gathering its power. Even though the summit was in sight, the day was half gone and the weather was deteriorating. As is our custom, we made the decision to descend and return to our base camp before the storm hit. Joe was furthest along toward the summit and decided to leave the safety of the rock bank and glissade down a high snowfield to where Don and I were standing on the rock. Using his ice axe as a brake, he used the snow like a children's slide and rapidly dropped to our elevation, stopping himself by digging his ice axe into the snow in a climber's arrest position. Newt was next on the climb and he too decided to glissade down. He smoothly descended until he was parallel with Don and me and stopped himself. I suggested that we tie into the rope now for our descent, but before any of us could move Newt slipped. Surprised by the suddenness, he fell from his secure position, shot down the slope and lost control of his ice axe in the process. As I watched him fall I was sick with fear. I knew the snow chute below was much steeper, with huge granite boulders at the base. I assumed the worst; I knew he would be seriously injured at best, could easily die, and, depending on which way he slid, I was not sure we could even recover his body. I was the designated leader on this climb and I watched one of our team fall to his probable death. Don and I quickly tied into our rope and jumped on the snowfield glissading down after Newt. Joe followed.

God was watching over Newt on this trip. He did enter the snow chute and fell steeply down into the field of boulders, bouncing some 15 feet through the rocks. He was bruised black and blue from neck to toe, but miraculously had not hit his head. His arm was gushing blood where it had been punctured by his ice axe, but no bones were broken. He was stunned and too deeply in shock to walk. After determining that nothing was broken, Don and I tied him into the rope and using ice axe belays we lowered him down the glacier over the next four hours arriving at camp for a late dinner. We kept him warm and fed him liquids all night and he rested. In the morning we carried his pack and equipment, but sore from head to toe, Newt slowly walked out the ten miles to his car and slept much of the drive home. His wife Susanna took one look at him and exclaimed: "That's the last time you go out with those guys!" But now, twenty years later and seventy-three years old, Newt still is an active member of the team.

Team members are responsible for their own conditioning, equipment, experience, and competence. But when they are accepted onto a team, the team – everyone – accepts responsibility for their care and development. An effective team is a place where members are encouraged to grow – where it is safe to risk learning – because the team is there to back them up. That's what the rope is all about. When one falls the rope means that everyone else is there to hold that person secure until he or she can get back on his or her feet. It is true in the office and on the mountain.

The story about Newt has become part of the lore of our mountaineering team for two reasons: first for the mistake and second for the response. The mistake was stepping onto the summit snowfield without being tied to a rope team. If Newt had been roped to Don and me at that moment, we could have arrested his fall and saved him from injury. The rope is the relationship that holds us accountable for our actions, but protects us from our mistakes. And it was the rope that made the rescue response possible. Don and I could move rapidly knowing we were roped to one another. And once we tied Newt into the rope we could lower him safely down the mountain to the care that he needed. The rope is the lifeline of the mountaineering team. The relationships among members are the heartbeat of any effective team.

Team members accept responsibility for the vision and values that make them a team

Membership on a team expands the capabilities of the individual members, but it also increases the scope of their responsibility. Each member is responsible for his or her own development and contribution, but, in addition, membership on a team implies acceptance of the team vision and values and responsibility for results. Team objectives take precedence over individual objectives. Team values, reflected in the accumulated culture, shape individual behavior. One of the strengths and challenges of teamwork is the reality that members must accept responsibility for their own contribution and at the same time own every other member's contribution and accept accountability for the goals of the team.[39] Teams expect broad ownership from their members, and perhaps this is why an effective team can accomplish so much. The objectives of the team transcend the aspirations of any one member.

Last year our mountaineering group gathered for our annual fall trip into the California Sierras. Six of us backpacked cross-country to a wonderful meadow we discovered years ago in the Cottonwood Lakes basin. The objective of this trip was to climb Mt. Langley, one of the 14,000-foot peaks on the Sierra Crest. The three-mile hike to camp is not strenuous, but the ascent up Mt. Langley is. The climb is not technically challenging, but it relentlessly climbs over New Army Pass and up the Pacific Crest to the summit. Years ago, Newt, Don, and I had made this climb. Don, however, had developed severe altitude sickness and stopped around 12,000 feet. Since he could wait in a public place and track our ascent visibly, he chose to stop there and read while Newt and I completed the climb.

This time all six of us started out early from camp, but at New Army Pass, Dwyer realized that his recent back surgery had not healed enough to tackle this trail. Newt and Rich decided they were not in as good physical condition as they wished. With six men we could safely create two teams. Dwyer, Rich and Newt chose to explore the Cottonwoods Basin, fish, and relax. Don, Brent, and I continued toward the summit. Somewhere beyond 13,500 feet, however, I began to feel the impact of altitude and decided I would keep them in sight but stop at the foot of the final rock ridge. Don and Brent continued to the top. The team objective was attained, but only because four of us chose to withdraw so that the stronger members could complete the climb. Team accomplishment took priority over our individual desires to stand on the summit.

Climbing Mt. Langley, of course, is only a weekend objective. That goal by itself did not require all six participants to make it possible for Don and Brent to reach the summit. They could have climbed it without the team. Expeditions to the major mountains of the world carry my point with more power. When Doug Scott and Dougal Haston climbed Mt. Everest in 1975, the world acknowledged their accomplishment and they went on tour celebrating the achievement. I met Doug Scott and saw his slides of the trip when he came through Southern California. It was a major accomplishment to forge a new route up the South West Face of Everest, but Doug Scott will be quick to tell you that they achieved that summit because 120 Sherpas, porters, cooks, doctors, and climbers participated in that climb. And the leader of that expedition, Chris Bonington, did not reach the summit on that trip. His job was to choreograph the decisions necessary to put a climbing team on the summit. Every other member of the team also had an important role in moving the expedition up the mountain until Scott and Haston were in place to reach the summit.[40] On effective teams, the purpose of the team takes priority over the agenda of the individual members.

This is not always easy for team members to accept. On October 15, 1978, Irene Miller and Vera Komarkova, with two Sherpas, stepped onto the summit of Annapurna, 26,545 feet high in the Himalayan mountains of Nepal. It was a moment of celebration. For months these two women, with eight colleagues under the leadership of Arlene Blum, had planned and advanced the necessary stages to place a climbing team on Annapurna's peak. Blum's expedition was the first American expedition to climb Annapurna and the first team of all-female climbers to ascend one of the world's 8000-meter mountains. With the help of their Sherpa guides, the expedition had succeeded. Arlene Blum was monitoring things from camp three ... and she was excited! It had been hard, but her dream was finally accomplished. As the expedition had moved up the mountain, the altitude and weather had taken their toll. Only four climbers still had the strength to even think about climbing beyond camp four. But the first team had made it. Miller and Komarkova with their two guides had reached the summit. Blum contacted the backup team at camp four and gave them the news. Good News!! The expedition was a success! But the Sherpas advised against a second team attempt, so Blum called everyone down from the mountain with thanks and celebration. For the two women waiting at camp four, however, this was not good news. While Alison Chadwick and Vera Wilson celebrated the success of the expedition, it was not enough to be part of the team that had put two women on top of Annapurna. They each wanted to be one of the women who reached the summit. And that personal objective clouded their judgment. Ignoring the advice of the Sherpas, they decided to try for a secondary summit on the side of Annapurna – one that had never been climbed. They roped up and headed for camp five – without the rest of their team. They never made it. Somewhere below the high camp they lost their footing and fell to their deaths. Another successful expedition marred forever by tragedy.[41] Effective teams are not collections of great members. Rather they are communities of persons committed to forming great teams. The team objectives shape the actions of its members, not the other way around.

Coming back to our climbing team at Mt. Langley, it is important to recognize that many teams have multiple objectives. Our group gathers annually for a long weekend trek, partly to climb another mountain but also to reconnect with one another and engage each other around important issues in our lives. That objective requires all seven men to be present. While only two of us pursued the summit objective to the end, all of us participated in the community conversation. This relational community with peers convened over thirty years is a high value for our group and has become one of our team objectives. Our actions together seek to pursue the shared vision of exploring wilderness *and* experience the shared values of deep long-lasting friendships. This is the commitment that keeps us active over the years, the rope that belongs to all of us.

Responsibility is a shared experience

Everyone on a team is responsible, and the rope makes that visible. Team members are responsible for themselves, their contribution, and their development. They are on the team because the team needs and wants them. It depends on them. Team members are accountable to the team for their contribution and their development. A member who cannot carry his or her own weight is a liability to the team, a drag on the rope. The strength *and* the weakness of teams is that the actions and attitudes of each individual member impact the effectiveness of the team as a whole.

> At its core, team accountability is about the sincere promises we make to ourselves and others, promises that underpin two critical aspects of teams: commitment and trust. By promising to hold ourselves accountable to the team's goals, we each earn the right to express our own views about all aspects of the team's effort and to have our views receive a fair and constructive hearing. By following through on such a promise, we preserve and extend the trust upon which any team must be built.[42]

And team members are responsible for the effectiveness of the team – for its shared vision and its lived values. Members invest in one another as they work for the health and success of the team – its relationships and its results. And like other forms of community, when a team is nurtured, it cares for the people that comprise it. Effective teams take care of their members, create

> When we are roped together everything we do matters

space for them to learn, grow, and develop because the strength of the team is tied to the strength of each member. The rope constrains us and it encourages us. It is the connection that defines the team and shapes its accountability. Everyone on the team owns the rope.

Questions for reflection

- Who owns your rope?

- For what are you responsible?

- For what is the team responsible?

- How does your contribution serve team responsibility?

- To whom are you accountable?

- Who asks you the questions that keep you focused?

- What does your accountability look like?

- To whom is the team accountable?

- What does team accountability look like?

- How does your vision fit with the team purpose?

- What are you promising?

Chapter 4

Who has the map and compass?

Teams require shared leadership

The delegation of leadership

In William Golding's classic story, *Lord of the Flies,* a leaderless group of boys stranded on a wilderness island evolved their own system of authority symbolized by the conch. Whoever held the conch was granted authority to lead and used that power for good and for evil. The holder of the conch was the leader.[43]

Within our mountaineering team, the symbols of leadership are the map and the compass. Everyone is expected to carry these navigational tools as part of the ten essential items basic for every trip.[44] The leader, however, will bring map and compass and complete understanding of the team destination, the route we will take, the difficulties involved, the time required, the equipment needed, and the assignments to be delegated. This is his job. It is the assignment we delegate to the leader.

Don was the delegated leader for our trek into the Virginia Lakes. We agreed on a date and asked Don to propose a destination to explore. He suggested a trip into Virginia and Matterhorn Canyons and we agreed. He did the research, planned each day's route, and suggested assignments of food and common gear. The rest of us shopped and packed as required and we convened at the trailhead on a warm October afternoon. The trek was a point-to-point trail over several mountain passes totaling 13,000 feet of elevation gain and loss. This meant positioning cars at both exit and entrance. Because this required an eight-hour drive to the trailhead, we started the trip later in the day than most of us would have liked. Late in the week at the end of a day, most of us were tired before we began. But it was a beautiful day in a magnificent piece of Sierra wilderness. The Virginia Lakes region is known for its awesome beauty.

Strapping on our packs we started up the trail toward Summit Lake. It felt steep. We had gone little more than a mile when one member of the team asked if the whole trail was like this. After hearing Don's answer he decided to drop out of the trip and take one of the cars home. Because we were so close to the cars the team agreed and he left us. We stayed on the ridge, however, and watched until he had reached the car before we continued on to the first pass. When we crossed the Pacific Crest at Summit Pass and reached Summit Lake it was late and we were hungry and tired. As we set up camp it started to thunder, then rain, lightning, and hail. We were not pleased.

The next day we followed the trail in a long steep bone-jarring descent for six miles, rapidly losing our hard earned elevation. Reaching lower Virginia Canyon we realized that we had a long uphill climb before us to gain back our elevation. The ridgeline that still separated us from Matterhorn Canyon consisted of unrelenting switchbacks that climbed slowly upwards toward Miller Lake. The team began to grumble and Don admitted that he had not studied the map as closely as he usually would have and had depended heavily on a guidebook he had read. Together we all studied our maps and determined that the total trip was at least six miles longer than we had thought, with considerably more elevation gain and loss. More grumbling. We had some hard hiking ahead if we were going to finish this trip on our long weekend. But we had a choice – there was a fork in the trail. The planned route was steeply uphill for several more miles before we could set up camp for the night. The fork, however, offered an alternative. From here it was only 12 miles down to Tuolumne Meadows in Yosemite Park, with access to a phone booth from which we could arrange transportation back to our cars. We had a choice. We could push ourselves to complete Don's originally planned trip or we could take a leisurely new route, also in beautiful country, with time for exploratory side trips. The grumbling increased, a mutiny was emerging. The team called for a decision.

Don and I are two of the founding members of this team and it is very unusual for us to disagree, but this time we did. On this particular trip my knees were bothering me and the extra length of the trip with the unexpected elevation gain and loss did not excite me. I knew I was hurting, and listening to others I knew I was not alone. So we talked. We did not ask Don to decide. That is not the authority we delegate to the leader. Decisions rest with the team. Responsibility rests with the team. The leader is accountable to see that we make the necessary decisions and act on them. So with our leader we discussed our options in detail and called for a rock vote.

The rock vote is a model for decision-making that we adopted early in the formation of our team and it has proved useful over the years. When a team decision needs to be made the options are clarified and each team member has five votes – five rocks (or fingers) to vote toward the options. We have found this method useful because it allows people to vote their preferences without negating the alternatives. Normally when two options are on the table team members will vote their rocks 3–2 in favor of one option. If a person feels strongly about an option they may vote 4–1. It is rare that a person votes his rocks 5–0 since that implies no worth at all in the alternative. This model of deciding has become so embedded in our culture that a person who votes 5–0 very often will not be invited back on the team. A 5–0 vote in our mind does not give the team credit. And in a team, which takes 3–2 and 4–1 votes seriously, a 5–0 vote can skew the outcome. It gives too much weight to the individual. Two men who joined the mountaineering team during past years voted 5–0 consistently. At first the group did not want to include them in the decision-making process. Then we decided not to include them on the trips. Team voting acknowledges that every option was proposed because it has value in someone's mind. Most of us have used variations of the rock vote in our work settings and with our families and find it a useful tool.

I think the Virginia Lakes trip was one of the only times I have voted 4–1. I did feel strongly about the choice. I thought we should not attempt the original trip that Don planned. However, when the vote was counted we had a tie and that was enough to cause me to reconsider. I changed my vote to 3–2 and we continued our planned itinerary, climbing steeply to the ridge summit.

On the summit I suggested that we take a short excursion up a prominent knoll. From this vantage point we had a spectacular view of Tenaya Lake, the rounded domes of Yosemite National Park and craggy peaks of the Cathedral Range – nice payback for the hard work. Buoyed by the magnificence of this view we continued down the ridge to Miller Lake, a high Sierra jewel tucked away in a natural west-facing bowl. Steve and I took a quick swim to wash off our lethargy. Don and Brent tended their blisters and Dwyer fished. It was a refreshing break and encouraged our spirits. The rest of the trail proved as long and as steep as we feared but it was quite beautiful. When we reached the car on Sunday afternoon we were glad that we had completed the full 35 miles, but we knew that we had stretched our physical condition unwisely and we were very glad that the weather had not been worse to complicate the trek.

Don was the delegated leader. It was his assignment to know how far, how long, and how steep the trail would be. He was quick to admit that he did not give sufficient attention to these details. Of course with a successful outcome the team was quick to forgive, especially since we all knew that we individually and corporately were responsible with access to the same maps and information that Don used. The team delegated the assignment but not the responsibility. And the team took back that delegation when it needed to decide. *Team leadership is more intimate than ordinary organizational leadership.* The relationship between leader and follower is much closer; the leadership is shared and moves frequently back and forth between leader and team. The team delegates specific assignments to a leader, but it does not delegate responsibility for its results. The team ultimately is the leader. The rope makes that visible.

Leadership on a rope team

On our rope teams – literal and virtual – the leader is the organizing agent, the member assigned responsibility to coordinate our combined efforts toward the accomplishment of our objective. Usually the team selects the leader for a specific climb or trip. Occasionally one person has a trip in mind and proposes it. Those who wish to participate then form a team in response. Whether the initiative begins with one member or with the collective team, it always rests on the choice to join, the decision to participate, and the willingness to assign leadership responsibility to the designated person. The leader accepts the delegation from the team and distributes responsibilities back to the other members.

Leadership on a rope team is an assignment. It is about service to the team not about being the leader. On a rope team everyone is a leader. You are not invited to clip into the rope if you do not bring a high level of competence and confidence. Everyone has leadership potential and at one time or another everyone exercises leadership, influencing the decisions and behaviors of the team. The leader facilitates decisions; the leader does not make them. The team makes decisions. We expect the leader to know where we are going and keep that objective before us. The leader coordinates the assignment of responsibilities – leadership – to the other team members and makes sure everyone is informed and involved. The leader – and, we believe, everyone else on the team – makes sure that the weakest member is heard and cared for.

Leadership is shared. This happens in a variety of ways. Leadership rotates among team members from trip to trip. Don was leader for the trip to Virginia Lakes; Brent was leader for the Wonderland Trail; I led the Mt. Ritter climb. Any one of us could be the designated leader on any trip. However, we believe strongly that *one person* must be given the responsibility. Teams need accountable delegation and they need to make decisions; we like one person to attend to these processes – not to do the work or make the decisions – but to hold us accountable to be sure the team does the work and makes the necessary decisions.

Stacy Allison, the first American woman to reach the summit of Mt. Everest, recalls her experience on an attempt to climb the world's tallest mountain in 1987. She signed on with an expedition lead by Scott Fischer, the co-owner of Mountain Madness, a Seattle based guide service. Scott recruited a team of strong leaders, organized everything in preparation and facilitated all of the arrangements up to the Mt. Everest Base camp. From that point on, however, he decreed that he would not be the expedition leader – that team members were all strong leaders and did not need to be led. He would be the designated leader for official purposes but on the mountain he would have no authority; he would be one of the climbers.

In declaring himself a nonleader, Scott had created a leadership vacuum. Without a strong hand to direct our team, we lost confidence, trust, and respect in each other. We felt little obligation to contribute and help one another. The easiest thing was to concentrate on one's own advancement and to act out of self-interest, not in pursuit of a common agenda. The idealism of Seattle had fallen apart in the crucible of the Himalayas, and mighty Everest had yet to even test us … Without leadership, we lacked unity of purpose; and without that, the results were predictable; unclear priorities, misdirected efforts, ineffective utilization of resources and turf wars.[45]

The expedition failed. Scott Fischer was so focused on reaching the summit himself that he did not keep the group focused on its purpose, nor did he facilitate its decision-making processes. It was a year later with another expedition that Stacy Allison finally reached the summit of Mt. Everest. Even a team of leaders needs a leader to serve them. With a team of capable, confident, and independent leaders, someone needs to keep us focused on what we are doing together.

Leadership also changes hands within a trip for our team. When we arrive at camp, the person responsible for cooking leads out in meal preparation. The person assigned the tents influences how the camp is set up. When we rope up for an ascent, usually the strongest climber takes the lead, but with a team of strong climbers, different people take turns in leading. Task, competence, and willingness to serve the team determine who will lead at each stage of the trip.

When the climb is off-trail the leader chooses the route. Even then, with a knowledgeable team, others will suggest alternatives if they come to mind because everyone has a vested interest in the outcomes. But good teams do not allow members to follow their own paths. We follow the leader we have chosen. Unless the team takes back the leadership by vote, the designated leader chooses the route and we follow whether or not our suggestion has been accepted. When climbing through deep snow, the leader has to "cut trail," stomping down the snow to create a path for those following. That can be hard work and we take turns leading to share this tiring task. On steep climbs, the leader is the most exposed person. If others on the rope team fall, the leader can hold them secure before they fall far. However, when the leader falls, he or she will fall the length of the rope to the next person before the second person can hold them secure. Leading is the riskiest position in climbing. The leader, even more than other members of the team, is dependent upon the rest of the team for safety and success.

Leadership on a rope team always belongs to the team. One person may be delegated with leadership responsibilities for a particular trip or assignment, but that person is simply one member of the team with his or her particular assignment. The leader is not "above" or in any way set apart from the other members of the team. Rather, like every member of the team, the leader is a participating, contributing member who just happens to have the assignment of leader for a particular purpose. The gap between the leader and the others is no greater than that between any other members. This is another way in which teams differ from work groups. There is no hierarchy within teams. Even if the team is accountable to a larger expedition or organization, the team functions as a single integrated unit, sharing leadership among its members. True teams have a high level of intimacy in relationships of mutual dependence. Leadership is one of many delegations of trust offered by the team.

Leadership is a relationship of influence

People have been defining leadership for years. The variety of technical and anecdotal definitions is extensive and often more confusing than clarifying. Gary Yukl, in *Leadership in Organizations*, defines leadership as "the influence process whereby intentional influence is exerted by the leader over followers."[46] Paul

Hersey and Kenneth Blanchard, in their classic text *Management of Organizational Behavior,* see leadership as any attempt to influence the behavior of an individual or group, regardless of the reason.[47]

Leadership at its core is a relationship between two people. Even in a group or organizational setting where we may be responsible for leading a number of people, we are still leading within specific relationships. Leader and follower are two people engaged in a relationship. That is the context of leadership. Leadership is always about influence and it always happens in relationship. *Leadership is a relationship of influence in which one person seeks to influence the vision, values, beliefs, attitudes, or behaviors of another.* It is an intentional relationship with a purpose – a relationship of influence.[48] Leadership is not about a person or a position. It is about influence and it happens in relationships. With this definition it is clear that everyone exercises leadership at some time – everyone seeks to influence the thinking or actions of those with whom they are in relationship.

Seeing leadership as relationship rather than position embraces two other realities important to team leadership: first, leadership flows from the character of a person; and second, leadership is grounded in the perception of the follower. Research by James Kouzes and Barry Posner has underlined the fact that people follow leaders who are credible, who have integrity or character. By integrity or character they mean three things: personal values or beliefs; competence – the ability to turn our words into actions; and trust – confidence in our ability to do what we believe.[49] Character is more than stated beliefs and values. Character is something that emerges from within; it comes from the soul. It represents those deeply held beliefs or value commitments that shape who we are, that control all that we do. What we *say* is important becomes our stated values. What we *believe* is important, however, is always revealed in our actions, our behaviors.[50] *Behavior communicates character.* Integrity is the alignment of our stated beliefs and our behavior. We are influenced by persons whose character we respect, whose integrity we trust. And any influence that we attempt when we seek to exercise leadership flows from the character that shapes who we are. Our leadership flows from our core beliefs and values and shapes our relationships. Who we are matters, especially to those tied to our rope.

The second reality is frequently not given enough recognition. Leadership is perceived by followers. We can exercise every possible type of influence, we can have any title or delegated authority but unless someone chooses to accept that influence, we cannot lead. It is very important that those of us given responsibility to exercise leadership remember that our followers have choice and our leadership is always dependent upon their choosing to follow. In many ways, leadership rests in the hands of those who choose to follow. This is true in every organization but very visible and concrete on a rope team. *Unless the team chooses to follow, the leader does not go anywhere!* The leader is tied to the team. That may be the single most important truth to understand about team leadership. Leadership is a relationship of influence perceived by others who choose to follow. It is a delegation of trust given by the followers.

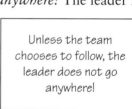

Unless the team chooses to follow, the leader does not go anywhere!

Leadership serves purpose and people

The delegation of leadership to one member of the team is an assignment to care about purpose and people. In his book *Leadership is an Art,* Max De Pree says that the two primary responsibilities of a leader are to point the direction or define reality and to say thank you. For De Pree, leaders articulate the vision; they point the direction and define the reality which shapes both the leadership relationship and the follower's contributions to the team. However, he recognizes immediately that the vision articulated by the leader will only be accomplished with the contributions of those followers. Thus, he sees the second responsibility of leadership as saying thank you – acknowledging dependence upon and appreciation for the followers and their personal investment in the vision.[51]

The responsibilities of team leadership always embrace two outcomes: the objective or mission of the team and the care and development of its members. [52] Leadership is a responsibility of service. It is a specific assignment given to keep the vision in view, point the direction, and clarify the issues at hand. Stacy Allison, the first American woman to climb Mt. Everest, led her own successful expedition to climb K2, the second highest summit in the world. She states emphatically: "The leader serves the people and organization by creating a clear focus, direction and purpose."[53] Leadership is also the assignment to keep an eye on the rope – the relationships that connect the members of the team and help or hinder their progress. The leader is responsible for the team as team.[54]

Each member is accountable for their particular contribution to the team, but the leader is attending to the connections among those contributions and the health of community within the team.

Leadership influence is defined by organizational expectations

Team leadership differs from traditional organizational leadership because of the intimacy of the relationships. Leadership at its core is a relationship of influence. That influence, however, is exercised differently depending on the organization's expectations for leadership. When leadership is being exercised by senior executives, the organization looks for influence about direction, vision, values, strategy, renewal, and change. When the leadership is coming from middle management, the organization expects influence toward stability, order, delegation, recognition, and empowerment, contextualizing each person's contribution within the larger vision. Both are expressions of leadership, but the organizational setting defines the purpose of the influence expected. Senior leaders tend to stand apart from those they lead, while middle managers are more likely to belong to the ranks of the followers they seek to influence.[55]

Team leadership, I believe, provides a third set of expectations. The team corporately owns the vision, direction and strategies and retains responsibility for change and renewal.[56] The team also is small enough to monitor its own order, recognition, and contextualization. The team expects its leader to facilitate the team's processes – its decisions, delegations, and measurements of success. The relationship between leader and followers in a team setting, therefore, is less structural and more intimate than the relationships of senior executives or middle management leaders. The relationships are much closer because the team leader is a participating member of the team. Again, the rope makes that visible.

The team is the leader

The close-knit nature of a small team of people makes it possible for everything to be shared including leadership. The team corporately is really the leader. The team delegates a coordinating, facilitating function to one of its members who is responsible to keep an eye on the team as a whole. But the team retains most of the authority of leadership.

The team owns the purpose and values

Everyone on the team participates in the selection of destination, strategies for achieving that objective and the competencies needed for success. In the early stages the values of the founding members shape the culture of the team, the character of the community formed by its network of relationships. Over the years, however, that culture takes on a strength of its own, shaping the selection of new members and defining the way the team works together. Everyone on the rope is heading toward the same goal with a common set of values and compatible beliefs. The vision and values are shared.

The team delegates shared leadership

The team collectively selects a leader to serve its progress toward the chosen objective. Certain responsibilities are given to the "leader" to facilitate team actions and represent the team if needed with outside persons or organizations. We expected Don to obtain the necessary wilderness permits and arrange where we would park our cars while in the backcountry. At the same time, the team expects the leader to share leadership responsibility by delegating specific assignments back to its members. Brent and I may be responsible for tents. Rich and Steve may be expected to take leadership with cooking. Dwyer and Newt may take care of transportation. Shared leadership is about "The transference of the leadership function among team members in order to take advantage of member strengths (e.g. knowledge, skills, attitudes, perspectives, contacts, and time available) as dictated by either environment demands or the developmental stage of the team."[57] Everyone contributes; everyone shares the leadership on behalf of the team.

The team makes decisions around comfort and commitment

When lives are at stake everyone has a vested interest in outcomes. An effective team owns its results and embraces high participation in decision-making. Organizations tend to avoid complete consensus decision-making because it distributes too much power to the negative vote. We believe, however, that the intimacy of team relationships makes consensus important. There is no space on a rope for someone who disagrees. Everyone has to be moving in the same direction or the team will not reach its destination. Consequently everyone has a voice and every voice is heard.[58] We move forward when everyone has agreed and is comfortable. The decision of when to rope up is made when anyone wants the security of the rope.[59] The decision to turn back is made when anyone decides he cannot go further. The weakest person on the rope always sets the pace for the rest of the team. Sometimes one person's limitation can be covered by another's strength. But that is only acceptable if both people feel comfortable about continuing forward. We use the rock vote as a tool for building consensus without having complete agreement. While we prefer complete consensus, we want at least comfortable commitment. The rock vote only works if members give consideration to others' points of views as well as their own. When we seek consensus, a 5–0 vote will almost always shape the outcome. And because of safety issues in the mountains it will always be honored, but perhaps that person should not have been on the team for that trip. We place a high value on consensus but use the rock vote to develop comfortable commitment, preserving team relationships even as we pursue team purposes.

The team resolves its conflict

Conflict is endemic to relationships. "All great relationships, the ones that last over time, require productive conflict in order to grow."[60] Conflict is not necessarily something that happens between persons. My psychologist friends say it happens within a person. It is the internal response we have when we encounter something different from what we expect or desire. Don and I have experienced these feelings of conflict often on the rope and in the canoe. Several are permanently implanted in my memory. I remember Don verbalizing his conflict loudly with the words "back-paddle, not draw!" We were riding a roiling cascade down a stretch of the Trinity River with a large rock directly ahead. Don, the experienced canoeist, sat in the stern because he did not trust my ability; he steered and directed what he needed me to do. I sat precariously in the bow, with cold water pouring into my lap and strong instinctive reactions concerning what I needed to do to survive. Don yelled "back-paddle" to pull us off the rock, but I was deep into a draw stroke, which felt like a much more proactive way to avoid landing on top of the rock. Two separate opinions about how to survive, but I was in front, I would hit first! Don, however, was right this time and responding to his conflict I changed strokes and we dodged the rock and sped on downstream. Then we talked about conflict, instructions, fear, and relationship.

I also remember the "green tongue." Once again we were negotiating the rapids further down the river. Don yelled to me to head between two rocks up ahead. Unfortunately from the back of the canoe he could not see that the river dropped off on the other side of the rocks. We shot through the gap riding a green tongue of water that poured over the edge like a fountain. I remember distinct feelings (and words) of conflict as I flew over the bow of the canoe watching it drop down the little waterfall while I sailed through the air and found myself bobbing downstream in the cold water. Once again we had a conversation.

Conflict is a natural part of developing relationships and it must be faced and dealt with. We have found that the sooner we talk about these feelings the sooner we can learn how to resolve them and move forward in the relationships. Whether it's stepping on the rope, failing to cook dinner, forgetting the tent stakes, misreading the map, misplacing the keys, or failing to communicate on the river, we talk about the issue, how we feel, what we can learn from it, and how we go forward together from here. If both the purpose and the relationships are important, conflict can be managed as a normal corollary to growth. When conflict is not faced, relationships are damaged and team objectives are clouded. After thirty years in the wilderness together every member of our team has had conflicted feelings in relationship with every other member of the team. We talk about it often. Because we are roped up, we have what my colleague Richard Gorsuch calls high trust and interlocking goals. The rope – the connective relationship – creates trust in place of anxiety and requires mutual dependence to achieve our purpose.[61] That is precisely why we are still climbing mountains together after thirty years.

The team gives and accepts delegation

Delegation is at the heart of the team. Everyone owns the outcomes, the results desired; and everyone accepts responsibility for an assignment that contributes to those outcomes. Delegation, Max De Pree says, is the gracious act of involvement.[62] It is the sharing of leadership, the giving of trust. Teams are built upon trust. Everyone accepts delegation and trusts everyone else to be as deeply committed. This is the beauty of teams. We carry the load together. The team chooses a leader and expects the leader to delegate the work right back to the team.

The leader is one member of the team

Leadership on an effective team is simply one of the assignments delegated. The leader is one member of the team. The map and compass – our wilderness conch – is held symbolically by one person but only as his work to be done in service to the team. The team is the leader. This is why everyone brings a map and compass.

Questions for reflection
- Who is following your lead?

- Why are they following?

- Whose lead are you following?

- Why do you follow?

- How do you measure performance and results?

- How do you measure relational maturity?

- How are decisions reached in your team?

- How is conflict managed in your team?

Chapter 5

"Belay on"

Teams create a safe environment for development

The belaying rope

My leg was shaking uncontrollably with what we call "sewing machine leg." There was no hiding the fact that I was afraid as I clung to the face of the rock. The toes of my boots perched precariously on the lip of a tiny ledge jutting from the rock. The fingers of my left hand were jammed into a small crack in the rock. My right hand grasped a knob of rock as I held my balance. Don was encouraging me to continue climbing up the rock face. My nerves were begging me not to move, to flatten myself against the rock and stay there. My mind knew I had to move; my leg was getting weak. Flattening against the rock was the most dangerous position I could take; it increased the likelihood I would fall.

We were in Joshua Tree National Park practicing. Part of the training we received in the Sierra Club's Basic Mountaineering Training Course included rock climbing. This has never been one of my favorite pastimes. Some people experience a great adrenalin rush and reinforcing excitement crawling up massive rock faces like human flies. Not me. I have the great adrenalin rush but it just reinforces my fear and increases the violence of shaking leg. Climbing, however, is a skill necessary for survival in wilderness travel. It is a skill that everyone on the rope team must have to ensure that they can climb out of any predicament they might find themselves in. So we learned and we practiced annually.

Again the rope played an important role. One person, in this case Don, would anchor himself in a secure position – usually seated comfortably, tied into a tree or rock behind him. The climbing rope was wrapped around him as a brake and held firmly in his hands taking up or letting out slack as needed by the climber. I tied into the other end of the rope for safety and selected a route up the rock face, looking for foot and handholds that might allow me to ascend to the top. When I was ready, I called out "On belay?" signaling Don that I was ready to climb and wanted to know that he was backing me up. Don answered, "Belay on," telling me that he was securely anchored, had the rope in hand and would protect me if I fell. There are other signals between climber and belayer but both parties know that the rope will be held secure until the climber calls, "Off belay," and the belayer replies, "Belay Off."[63]

Climbing is essentially a team sport, and the rope which joins the team is not only a symbol of its unity but also insurance for safe travel on steep rock, ice, and snow. The very act of roping up may instill confidence in an unsteady climber, but to have any value the rope must be used in such a way as to provide genuine security for all members of the team. The technique of providing this security is called *belaying* and its purpose is to reduce the length of a fall and minimize its consequences.[64]

With the belay set I started to climb. The belay rope always has some slack. It will not hold me in position or do my climbing for me; it is there to shorten my fall if I slip. Close to the ground I climbed well. However, about half way up I reached a spot that stopped me. My position felt very insecure and the next hand and foot holds seemed just out of reach. I was not confident I could stretch that far without falling, so I froze. And my leg started shaking. Don shouted encouragement to me from the other end of the rope. Other members of the team from the safe perspective of the ground below pointed out several possible routes I could take up the rock. None of this removed my fear but it did encourage me to try. So I chose my route and stretched tentatively toward the next handhold. And I fell. My fear became reality.

But Don was paying attention. When the rope snapped taut Don cinched down his belay and held my fall to a few feet. I dangled there, surprised but not hurt. The team safety precautions worked. The rope held. That knowledge released a new level of confidence – confidence in the team and the rope that translated into confidence about what I could do. While Don held the rope secure, I regained my footing on the rock and quickly returned to my earlier position. Now, however, trust replaced my anxiety and I stretched out confidently, knowing that Don would catch me if I fell. And I scampered up the rest of the rock face without hesitation. Jim Collins makes a distinction here between "fallure" and "failure." In "fallure" you fall while stretching for the next hold. Failure is not trying. It is giving in to your fear and letting go.[65]

The rope does not prevent the climber from falling but it shortens the fall and reduces the risk. I knew that before I started climbing. I had heard that in the Sierra Club course. I read about it in mountaineering books. But I had to fall before I truly believed it enough to risk climbing. A climbing team with a good rope and high trust creates the safe space needed to risk learning and growth.

Trusting the rope

The heartbeat of any team is trust. Trust is the essence of the rope – the relationship – that connects members. Without trust the relationship is weak. Without trust there is no leadership. Without trust we cannot get anything done together. Without trust there is no space in which to risk, to learn, to grow. *Trust is the acknowledgement of our dependence upon another.*[66] It is the willingness to place our dreams, visions, values, and even lives in hands we can't control. When I stood on the ledge and reached for the next handhold, I trusted Don to be attentive and the relationship visible in the rope to hold true. That is how teams work. High relationships of trust among members provide encouragement and confidence. Knowing that

> Trust is the acknowledgment of our dependence upon another

colleagues are committed to the same outcomes and care about us gives us a freedom to risk. It reduces the anxiety that builds up in a person when conflict, fear or simply the unknown hinders us from moving forward. Trust embraces vulnerability, the risking of self. And it risks failure; we might fall. Trust allows us to take those risks, to believe that a fall will not be fatal, that weakness and fear will not lose our respect or damage the relationship. The rope reminds us that the team surrounds us. The team shares our objectives and is there to help us learn how to succeed.

It is this high commitment to trust as foundational to team effectiveness that underlies the rock vote approach to conflict and decisions. Teams trust the members, listen to alternative possibilities, and willingly let colleagues influence outcomes.

> Knowing that trust is key, exemplary leaders make sure that they consider alternative viewpoints, and they make use of other people's expertise and abilities. Because they're more trusting of their groups, they're also more willing to let others exercise influence over group decisions. It's a reciprocal process. By demonstrating an openness to influence, leaders contribute to building the trust that enables their constituents to be more open to their influence. Trust begets trust.[67]

On an effective team, members trust the rope that connects them. The team offers a rock-solid belay to all members, encouraging them to risk growth for the sake of the shared objective. And the members of the team risk that personal development, knowing that they are cared for and the team will see that their risky growth does not prohibit the team from achieving its objective. The success of a team is directly proportional to its commitment to the growth and accomplishment of its members.

Embracing vulnerability

So how is trust built? How does a team develop the level of trust that encourages its members to risk failure to achieve growth? It starts with the leader in any organization. It starts with each person on a team. Giving trust is the first risk. And it starts with vulnerability.

Openness and trust are very closely related. Trust is manifested when one person chooses to reveal something of themselves that they would otherwise conceal. It requires a level of experience and affection among members of a group. Affective trust is based on limited but successful experience in sharing sensitive information with another, whereas resilient trust is developed over longer periods of successful interaction with the same person or group of people.[68]

Trust is built when we make ourselves vulnerable to others whose response we cannot control. We earn trust by giving trust. We receive trust from others as we demonstrate our trust in them. Trust is reciprocal; it is relational. And once again the rope is a concrete expression of that trust. It protects us because we are vulnerable.

I do not like to admit that I am afraid, that I have weaknesses or limitations. This is actually a serious problem for leaders. Our reluctance to reveal our fears, weaknesses, and limitations causes us to put up a strong front even though those who look to us for leadership know that we are human. They know that we have fear and weakness just like they do. Often they can see it in us whether we admit it or not. And yet so many leaders continue to hide their vulnerability. Recently in a seminar with CEOs I made the comment: "I am old enough now to realize that I am not the only person afraid of being found out." Everyone in the room sat up suddenly. And that started a conversation because everyone felt the same way. We all know our fears and weakness and we resist revealing them, concerned that others will think us weak and unfit for leadership. If we are weak we might not be able to influence the results for which we are accountable. Yet just the opposite is true. When we acknowledge our vulnerability, it places our trust in those around us and encourages them to trust as well.

When I stand frozen on a ledge with my leg shaking visibly it is rather obvious that I am afraid. My vulnerability is exposed for all to see. But that is when the team rallies. That is when rope and relationships do their work. With the team I can climb that rock face; by myself I would never attempt it. Teams require trust as the relational glue that holds them together and allows them to accomplish their goals. Trust embraces vulnerability that leans into the strengths of the team. And vulnerability includes the risk of failure.

Learning from failure

Kouzes and Posner picked up a wonderful quote: "Success does not breed success. It breeds failure. It is failure which breeds success."[69] The key is whether or not we can learn from our failures. Sooner or later we fall – we fail. The question is how we respond. If we can use that mistake as an opportunity for learning, then failure will always be productive. I have often heard Max De Pree say that leaders are right only half the time. That means that half the time we are wrong. We are mistaken; we fail. But that is how leaders learn. Teams can create a culture of learning that, while it does not encourage failure, embraces failure as a step toward knowledge and growth. The very nature of a team, with its interconnected relationships, provides a safety net for error. Teams are roped together; they cover for one another. They back one another up and hold each member secure when he or she stumbles and falls. An effective team may be the best place to fail because it has the resources to allow learning to emerge. The rope allows space to risk vulnerability, to learn from our falls. The rope is a symbol of forgiveness and freedom to try again.

Yet forgiveness is not a topic covered in many leadership books or manuals for team development. No one talks about forgiveness! This may well be the crisis of leadership today. I am becoming increasingly convinced that there can be no healthy relationship without forgiveness. Leadership requires forgiveness. Teams depend on forgiveness. And forgiveness nurtures leadership.

Now what do I mean by forgiveness? I am not talking about theology, even though the forgiveness of God is the foundational principle of Christian theology and the model for reconciliation and renewal in relationships. We are looking at people, human relationships, and organizational communities of interdependent people – teams. Leadership in human communities, I believe, is not possible without forgiveness. Forgiveness turns failure into learning.

Forgiveness acknowledges a person's failures and mistakes and takes them seriously but does not hold them against the person. In life, mistakes are natural; they are the byproduct of learning. I have always told my staff that they will make mistakes no matter how hard they try not to. That is normal. The objective is not to make the same mistake twice. Learn from it and move on to the next one. Failure, a big mistake, is a necessary corollary of leadership. Someone once defined leadership as making a decision when the alternatives are equal. I like that definition. Leadership is taking the risk of deciding when you do not know which choice is right. If you knew, there would be no risk. It would be obvious and there would be no need for leadership. Leadership is required when you don't know – when you must decide – when you take the risk – when you risk failure. By definition then, since no one is right all of the time, leadership will include failure. Failure is a necessary prerequisite to leadership. And on effective teams that leadership is shared. Teams distribute leadership and diffuse the impact of failure. On healthy teams, members cannot fail; only the team can fail. The team ropes together to accomplish a shared objective. That connectedness encourages risk, protects it from being fatal, and creates the space to learn from the experience and move forward. Forgiveness accepts failure and expects a person to have learned from his or her mistake. Forgiveness treats failures as educational milestones for leadership – which should make forgiveness the first leadership response to failure. It is forgiveness that turns failure into learning opportunities. It is forgiveness that nurtures the relationships that define the team.

Teams must create a context of forgiveness if they expect leadership to occur in their midst. Members must embrace their own vulnerability and offer forgiveness to one another if they want to contribute to that context of forgiveness and nurture the development of the team. Forgiveness is the most important gift a team can give to its members. It makes trust possible. It offers people the chance to take risks, to learn, and to grow in their own leadership within the team. Forgiveness is something we need, given our own vulnerability and it is something we must offer others, increasing our vulnerability and building trust.

Giving the belay

In 1989 Mark Wellman and Mike Corbett ascended El Capitan Peak in Yosemite Valley. After seven days of intense climbing on the massive rock face, the team emerged at the summit to be greeted by the news media. The event was heralded by radio, TV, and newspapers across North America. What was so special about this climb? Hundreds of climbers ascend the 3,000-foot face of El Capitan every year. The difference was in the climbers. Mark Wellman had attempted another climb in 1982 and had fallen 100 feet. He was permanently paralyzed from his waist down. He would never climb again. But Mark Wellman had a dream. He wanted to climb El Capitan. And Mark had a friend, a friend who believed in him, encouraged him, coached him, and invested the time and energy necessary to get Mark to El Capitan.

The news media celebrated the feat of Mark Wellman. We also need to recognize the role of Mike Corbett, the friend who tied himself to a paraplegic and encouraged him up one of the most daunting rock climbs in North America.[70] The relationship between Mark Wellman and Mike Corbett represents for me the essence of an effective team. Mark Wellman could not hide his weakness and failure. He had to live with it. Mike Corbett did not shun his crippled friend. Rather they roped up together, and together they overcame the limitations of Mark's weakness to grow together and accomplish their goal. In 1999 they repeated this climb, ascending the more difficult nose route in eleven days.[71]

Teams create space for members to take risks, learn, and grow because the other members of the team, roped together, offer a belay. The team provides the security of a solid anchor, a supportive context and the encouragement to move from vulnerability to growth. Good teams create safety. They provide space to learn. They achieve results together because they take care of one another. They listen, they encourage, they teach, they forgive, and they expect learning. A good team belays its members and asks for their best.

Mentoring one another

The belaying relationship of climbers on a rope is a striking metaphor for the powerful relationship of mentoring. Mentoring is a teaching-learning relationship between two persons focused on the development of one person but benefiting both. Much has been written about the importance of mentoring for personal renewal and development of leaders.[72] Men and women, recognizing their need to learn and grow, seek out other men and women who have experience, wisdom, or knowledge and invite them into their lives. Mentors walk portions of our life journey with us and ask us the questions that focus our learning and clarify our purpose. Max De Pree has been such a mentor in my life for over twenty-two years. He is a leader with whom I have been able to rope up as I explored my leadership journey. In many ways he has been a Mike Corbett to me.

Mentoring also occurs within teams. At its core, mentoring is an intentional learning relationship between two persons, where one or both persons share from their life and experiences the wisdom of their heart and mind and where one or both persons give the other the trust to hold them accountable to their stated vision and values. Mentoring is a powerful strategy for leadership development and personal growth. The parties involved determine the content, structure and timing of the relationship uniquely. I don't think there is one best model or one right model. What are important are trust, honesty, vulnerability, and a relationship of belonging, encouragement, affirmation, accountability, and hope.

I believe that some of the same benefits of the mentoring relationship – encouragement, affirmation, forgiveness, perspective, and challenge – can be found in small groups of persons committed to one another's learning and development. The rope team has played that kind of role on my journey, teaching me much about leadership, relationships, community, and life. Chilean climber Rodrigo Jordan put it well after reaching the summits of Mt. Everest and K2: "Friendship, mutual consideration, affection, humility, and caring about your teammates are not just important qualities: They are essential. These are the traits that allow a team both to perform at its peak and to reach a new dimension of satisfaction and joy in so doing."[73]

Thirty years of climbing mountains, sharing canoes, sleeping in snow caves, and belaying one another on rock faces give intimate insight into each other's lives. It is normal for members of our team to be in conversation by telephone or email – counseling, advising, coaching, and mentoring one another through our various responsibilities. There is much mentoring wisdom in the group, and we learn much about life and leadership from each other as well as in the organization and safe execution of a mountain climbing expedition. And, of course, there is a very high level of trust. "What is said on the trail stays on the trail." In a way, the group itself corporately becomes the mentor to each of its members as well as the context that sustains a network of valuable accountability relationships. In the team setting, we bring a diversity of life experience and age span to the relationships. We bring varied skills, knowledge, and passions. Because the team was formed around shared vision and shared values, we have common interests as well as shared concern for one another. Over the years, we have found that someone in the group has the wisdom, experience, or knowledge to talk us through a learning curve whether it be in the wilderness or at home. Three of us meet for lunch every Thursday, share the experience of our week, ask each other the questions we should be reflecting on as we review our lives, and consider the journey forward. We also enjoy each other's company and plan the next wilderness trip.

"Belay off"

The mentoring relationship – the belaying rope – provides a safe environment for development. When we know we are held securely we can take the risk to step off the ledge and stretch for the next place to stand. The team, however, does not do our climbing for us, does not excuse incompetence. The team expects the best; it depends on each person's contribution to achieve its intended results. The rope reduces the risk of learning but it does not replace it. Rather it creates space for learning. The team holds its members secure until they get back on their feet. Then they expect the person to climb, to reach the summit, and to provide a belay for the next person climbing. "Belay on" signals partnership and sharing of risk. "Off belay" indicates that "I am in a secure position and do not need a belay any longer."[74]

Now I can belay another. "Belay off" is the team's response acknowledging that it understands and now expects a strong contribution from the climber in whose development it has been investing. "Belay off, let's have dinner."

Questions for reflection

- Where is your growing edge? What generates fear within you? What do you need to learn next?

- When did you last fall? What did you learn from that failure?

- Where do you feel safe enough to risk failure?

- How do you encourage the risk of learning?

- How transparent and vulnerable are you?

- Where are you building trust?

- How forgiving is your team?

- How is your team growing in competence and capacity?

- How are you growing in competence and relational maturity?

- Who holds your belay? Who are your mentors?

- Who are you belaying? Who looks to you for mentoring?

Chapter 6

Chicken Montana

Teams build community

The trip

The alarm goes off at 4:30 a.m. I rouse sleepily, dress, grab my pack and cross-country skis, and go outside to wait for the ride. Even in Southern California it's dark and cold in the early morning. We drive to Dwyer's house and transfer our gear into his van. The van carries five men and equipment in one vehicle, allowing us to talk as a group while we drive to the trailhead. There is not much talk for the first hour. I usually try to sleep a bit more. Dwyer is driving and at least one person is talking to keep him awake.

By the time we reach Mohave everyone is awake, eager for the trip, and hungry. In the early years we always stopped at The Pancake House. Pancakes, eggs, bacon, and coffee – stuffing ourselves with food we would not carry into the mountains. In recent years, McDonald's has become the stop of choice for Egg McMuffin, hash browns, and juice. In the car and around the table we catch up with one another's lives: what's happening with work, family, children, grandchildren, church, and the other activities that occupy our time when we are not in the wilderness.

Filled with carbohydrates and protein, we shuffle off to the van, change drivers, and continue to Lone Pine for gas. Again the van is filled with conversation as we reminisce about past trips, revel in our successes, and laugh at our foolishness. Time flies as we banter and re-engage our corporate memory. Before we know it we're in Bishop for the mandatory stop at Schatt's Bakery. For thirty years we have been stopping at this bakery. It is a team tradition. Sitting in the patio we eat more pastries than we ever would consider in normal life and anticipate the trip ahead. This time we are going to ski over Mammoth Pass for the long weekend. We check that everyone brought the group equipment assigned and question one another about the personal gear that we're carrying and find out what we will be eating at camp. Bagging a few pastries to go, we check the weather conditions at the Inyo Forest Ranger Station and head up the Sherman grade into Mammoth Lakes. By now the conversation is ranging widely from personal pleasures to the depths of theology. There is never a dearth of topics to consider. Nothing is off limits. The discussion is energizing and often educational.

The car is parked at Tamarack Lodge. Everyone changes into trail clothes, rearranges their gear, and stops for lunch. Dwyer is famous for lunches. Since he chooses (and carries) tasty but heavy lunches, we regularly give him this assignment. We eat well, anticipating how long it will take us to reach the frozen lake where we want to camp. Once again filled with food, everyone puts on boots and skis and shoulders their packs. Then someone asks, "Who has the car keys?" A groomed trail leaves Tamarack Lodge, but we soon slide off into powdery snow and climb into the John Muir Wilderness, reaching our chosen campsite around 4:00 p.m. It doesn't always work out this way, but we like to set up camp and have dinner before dark. Dropping our packs, everyone changes their socks, pulls on a parka and some set up tents while others build the kitchen.

The "kitchen" is usually a four-foot square snow table trenched around all sides with bench seats compacted around the trench. This family style table becomes the primary gathering place for the team in camp. Those who have chair frames for their Thermarest sleeping pads set them up and lean back in luxury while the purists among us shake their heads at such concessions to comfort. The designated cook sets up the MSR stove and soon we have water boiling as we talk over the roar of the stove. The conversation continues to range broadly, often exploring academic topics, psychological issues, or global concerns posed by our educators, psychologists, and business leaders. And the cook prepares the Chicken Montana. Chicken Montana is symbolic. Years ago *Backpacker* magazine used to publish trail recipes recommended by other hikers. One day I found Chicken Montana and brought it on a trip. It has become a staple, partly because it is easy and filling and partly now because it is tradition. It is almost unthinkable that we would have a trip without Chicken Montana – a rice, soup, and canned chicken concoction we would never eat at home. In the mountains, however, everything tastes good, especially if it is warm. For thirty years over Chicken Montana we have talked about the questions of life. Chicken Montana cooking on the stove is more than a meal. It is an experience of community. The cook stove becomes the campfire and we gather around it and share the stories of our lives, what we are learning and where we are going. When the rope team, the hiking team, sits in a circle around the pot of Chicken Montana we are a community – we belong, what we have to offer is valued, who we are is respected, and who we are becoming is affirmed.

In the winter it gets dark early – and cold. Temperatures range from +20 to –11°F, depending on the year and location. When the stove goes off (to conserve fuel) conversation moves to the tents. It is not unusual for us to turn in for the night by 6:30 p.m. and sleep deeply and warmly over twelve hours. Dwyer and Steve may stay up later – Dwyer because he cannot sleep that early and Steve because he is an astronomer awed by the unhindered display of the galaxy. The rest of us sleep luxuriously until morning dawns and everyone gathers again around the cook stove where water is boiled for oatmeal and coffee cake is heated – another tradition. (The round Sara Lee Pecan Coffee Cake fits perfectly into the top of the three-liter pot with which we boil water.)

With breakfast complete, the day's outing begins. Wearing daypacks with lunch and emergency gear, we ski up the ridge and over Mammoth Pass, dropping down steeply into the valley where Reds Meadows Hot Springs thrives in the summer. In winter, the resort is closed; everything is covered with several feet of snow – except the hot springs. The hot springs bubble up in a marvelous pool, warm as a bath, surrounded by snow. Here

Dwyer brings out lunch. We all have pleasant memories of sitting in the hot springs, warmth soaking into our bones, eating the frozen oranges that Dwyer carried for lunch. Hard work to get there, but decadent luxury for lunch. And of course hard work to ski back up over the pass to return to camp.

This time I try something new for dinner – spaghetti with clam sauce. It tasted great at home when my wife made it. My version is another story. The noodles drain poorly and the clams don't cook completely. It is like eating a tasteless paste with chunks in it. The experiment is not well received. The team begins to compare me with Rich, who has never lived down the trip he brought dinner. Rich was in a hurry when he went shopping so he just pulled things off the shelf, threw them in his pack in their boxes without thought to a menu. When it was time for dinner, Rich got altitude sickness and went into the tent, leaving Don and me to sort out his food supply and imagine what we could cook with the miscellaneous items. We were not pleased. It was years before Rich was asked to bring dinner again. And the clam spaghetti relegated me to breakfasts for a while. But this is a forgiving team and a learning group. Everyone takes a turn at various meals and we continue to experiment as long as someone brings Chicken Montana.

After another evening of conversation over dinner, we sleep our twelve hours, awake to oatmeal and coffee cake and ski back to the van. The trip home repeats in reverse. The first stop is Schatt's Bakery, with pizza in Mojave. And the conversation continues all the way home, now more future oriented about life, work, relationships, and our next trip. Usually we have the next trip planned and a leader chosen by the time we get home. The leader will determine who brings the Chicken Montana.

Teams are relational communities

For thirty years, the trip just described was the template for every wilderness outing of our team. Some were longer, some shorter. Some were climbs, some hikes, some canoeing, and some cross-country ski trips. Geography varied as well, from British Columbia to California, up and down the west coast from desert to mountain to seashore. But the basic pattern was familiar and two critical components were constant: food and conversation. Whatever we did, wherever we went, we talked – we ate together and we talked about the questions of life. We were building community, because effective teams are relational communities.

> Teams form first around purpose: shared vision, common objectives. That is the unifying reason for the existence of the team. But it is the relational connections between members that make a group of people an effective team.

Leadership texts talk about the dual responsibilities of leadership: achieving the mission and developing the people.[75] Nowhere is that more evident than in the life of a team. Teams are formed to achieve specific results, intentional outcomes. Purpose defines the direction and determines the membership of the team. But a team is a network of relationships, a relational community. The health of that community has a direct impact on the success of its mission. The relational side of the team needs as much attention as the purpose side. When a community of people respect, trust, and encourage one another the team objectives are more likely to be achieved.[76]

> A community forms and grows from the power of respect and trust in a group… This community embodies a quality of group interaction that goes beyond highly efficient teamwork, although it includes the best of what teams could be. It works in a creative way that supports the aspirations and development of the people in the group. It is inclusive and perceives everyone as a potential leader. It provides a safe place where people can make mistakes and be vulnerable without fear and with benefit to all. People communicate in an open and frank way and move toward consensus in making decisions. All types of love can flourish within communities of this type.[77]

Community sets teams apart from workgroups

An effective team recognizes the interdependence among its members as they work for the common objective and attend to the social side of its reality. Teams are communities of people – networks of relationships. And team relationships need to be nurtured and tended just like any other human relationships. Relationships, like most living things, are subject to entropy. If they are not tended, they deteriorate. That makes attending to the social dimension of the team important, and breaking bread together is a good place to start.

Sharing a meal together is an important part of relationship building.[78] I schedule as many of my mentoring and coaching sessions as possible over a meal. Eating together reinforces the relationship, even as we discuss together an objective agenda. It is not accidental that our mountaineering team spends so much time around food. This is where we build the intimate relationships that will sustain us when the rope is strained on a difficult climb. Anthropologist Sherry Ortner has been studying Sherpas and their relationships with Himalayan mountaineering expeditions for forty years. In her superb book, *Life and Death on Mt. Everest*, she notes the importance of the social dynamics within a team.

> Once the group gets to the mountain, differences of personality, nationality, climbing values, and many other things are enormously magnified by the close quarters, the stressful physical conditions, and the difficulty of the task. Although physical abilities, technical skills, and equipment are fundamental to success, the job of climbing the mountain involves as well an enormous component of interpersonal relations.[79]

We eat together and talk together deliberately to nurture the relationships among us, to multiply relationships throughout the team and thus to strengthen the rope that connects us in the wilderness. There is something about a shared meal, going back to the biblical concept of breaking bread together, that lowers defenses and opens communication at deep and personal levels. For some reason, eating makes talking more personal. And it feeds the relationships that build community.

Building community is the second goal of a team

Building community is one of the goals of an effective team. Since community contributes to the success of the team's outcomes, it becomes an objective in its own right. The relationships of community create the social capital that supports the team enterprise. Effective teams seek to achieve their intended results *and* build a community of intimate relationships. However, community building is always the secondary goal. The purpose of the team is its reason to be. Community is a necessary byproduct of shared vision, shared values, and shared leadership. It is always subordinate to the purpose, a means to the end. However, it is such an important part of the process of being a team and achieving the purpose that it deserves to be pursued as an appropriate second goal of the team. This is an important distinction.

During the twelve years I was president at Regent College, a graduate school affiliated with the University of British Columbia, I noted that applicants for employment tended to fall into two general categories. One group was energized by our mission and wanted to participate and contribute to that purpose. Another group saw the community spirit for which we were known and wanted to join that community. I soon learned that the first group would enhance our ability to achieve the mission and benefit from and contribute to the community as a byproduct of working together. The second group tended to be more interested in belonging and being taken care of than contributing to the purpose of the college. They could actually be a liability in pursuit of the mission. Purpose is the defining goal of the team, but a good team will build strong community in the pursuit of its purpose.

What is community?

Simply defined, a community is a group of people in the same place agreeing to live under the same set of laws or values. From that foundation, definitions vary from group to group depending on the purpose, beliefs, or values involved. I want a bit more than geography and rules from my concept of community. I like to think of community as *a network of relationships within which I belong, I can make a contribution, I will be valued, and I will grow*. That kind of community represents the relational dimension of team for me.

Community is about belonging

We are relational beings, created by relationship for relationship. It is in our DNA. We are social by nature and we have a deep need to belong. This is good and bad. Jean Lipman-Blumen, in her brilliant study of toxic leaders, asks why we choose to follow bad leaders. She sees part of the answer in an intense basic human need for belonging, for membership in a community that gives meaning and worth to our lives.[80] We look for community. We want to belong. We spend most of our life trying to understand where we fit into the story of this world – where we belong. Our life has meaning as we connect with others to accomplish something together.

Community is about contributing

That is why I preferred to appoint persons who looked to the mission before they looked to the community. Community only happens when we give ourselves, when we invest our gifts and abilities in others and the shared vision that unites us. Community is built on relationships of trust. And trust is given before it is earned. Community is where we belong precisely because we can make a contribution.

> It is up to each of us, therefore, to claim our place by focusing on that which sustains and renews us. We do this by recognizing what we have to offer to our communities and figuring out the best way to share it. In so doing, we make ourselves a resource for success in our communities and thus carve out the place in which we belong.[81]

The meaning, value, and worth of our lives becomes evident in community because who we are and what we have to offer contributes to something greater than ourselves. We are dependent upon one another, and that dependence requires something from everyone on the team. Everyone has a role to play for relationships to thrive and community to flourish. Once again, the rope makes that visible.

Community is about being valued

One of the benefits of community is that the very act of investing ourselves in others results in our being valued. Community is a place where we are respected, valued, and cared for. It is a place where we have our needs met in the process of meeting others' needs. I like to think that community goes beyond valuing the person for the contribution they can make to cherishing them for who they are. Teams form for a purpose, and that purpose requires a contribution from each member. Working together in pursuit of the shared purpose builds community, an intimacy of relationship in which members are respected for their contributions and valued for themselves. On a team, my contribution will be missed if it is not there; in community I will be missed. This respect and valuing draws contribution, illustrates belonging, and supports the mission of the team.

Community is about growing

Leider and Shapiro, in their wonderful little book *Claiming Your Place at the Fire*, recognize that we learn from our dependency. Tying into a rope team is a palpable demonstration of trust, an acknowledgment of dependency. We need one another in order to succeed. In this position of need we tend to be more tuned for learning. Dependency opens the mind to limitation, mortality, and options. Being dependent on another – not being able completely to take care of our self – can be a transformative experience for both persons. When we reveal our need, we allow another to help and that too is a fundamental human need – to help others find their place in the world. Dependence focuses the mind on what is important – our need and our need to be needed.[82] Community is about learning and growing together. When we belong and contribute we grow with the community. Communities learn and develop with the addition of new members or the benefit of new experiences. The corporate wisdom of the community should be continually increasing and an effective team will expect its members to build on that wisdom. Participation on a good team, belonging to an intimate community, increases the capacity of each member.

Community cultivates reflective questions

This is how wisdom develops. An effective team, a relational community lifts up the questions that need to be examined. Communities talk a lot about everything. On the trip template described above, I hinted at an agenda of conversation. From Pasadena to Mojave, we catch up with one another's lives, what is happening with work, family, children, grandchildren, church, and the other activities

Questions of community
• Who am I?
• Where do I belong?
• What do I care about?
• What is the purpose of my life?
• Who am I becoming?
• Why are we doing this?

that occupy our time when we are not in the wilderness. This begins to get at the fundamental question of life: Who am I? From Mojave to Bishop we reminisce about past trips, revel in our successes, and laugh at our foolishness. In this process of remembering together our corporate history we solidify our sense of community: Where do I belong? Remembering rekindles relational connections. From Bishop to Mammoth we explore: What is important? What do I care about? Here, with conversation ranging from personal pleasures to profound theology, we explore the passions of our lives, the legacy we want to leave, the heart of God that we want to have. Around the cook stove at night we wrestle with eternal questions of theology and philosophy: Why am I here? What is the purpose of my life? And on the trip home we look forward: Who am I becoming? Who do I intend to be? What do I need to learn next? The conversations explore the choices before us in life, work, and relationships and begin the process of setting up the next trip.

Of course, this agenda is artificial. It happens on every trip but not necessarily in the neat order of my template. And we talk on the trail as well as around food and in cars. Trail talk adds to the mix – discussion of destination, strategy, purpose, and accomplishment of the team objective: Why are we doing this? The team objective is always before us but we take the community dimension seriously. I don't think we have ever taken a trip into the wilderness when our conversation did not range over all of the topics just listed. This is why we look forward to being together. It is why we have been together for thirty years. And it is why we have climbed as many mountains, explored as many wilderness areas, and swamped as many canoes as we have. Teams are relational communities. Effective teams build and nurture strong communities.

Building community

So how do we build community? Several suggestions emerge from our years as a rope team:

Fireside reflection

Leider and Shapiro look to the way wisdom is distributed in African tribal culture. Elders sit close to the fire and tell the stories of their lives, reflecting on what they have learned in a way that others can benefit from.[83] Sitting around a fire and reflecting has long been a way that people have learned from and shared their experiences. We do not build fires in the wilderness for environmental reasons. But the cook stove, the car ride, or the restaurant meal provide adequate opportunities to stop and reflect, to think about our life journey – where we have been and where we are going. Warren Bennis thinks reflection is the major way we learn from the past. Telling our stories forces us to look back, think back, draw conclusions from the connections, and invite others to mine our story for nuggets we have missed.[84] Kouzis and Posner put it well:

> Simply put, you have to teach others your vision. Teaching a vision – and confirming that the vision is shared – is a process of engaging constituents in conversations about their lives, about their hopes and dreams. Remember that leadership is a dialogue, not a monologue. Leadership isn't about imposing the leader's solo dream; it's about developing a shared sense of destiny. It's about enrolling others so

that they can see how their own interests and aspirations are aligned with the vision and can thereby become mobilized to commit their individual energies to its realization. A vision is *inclusive of constituents'* *aspirations; it's an ideal and unique image of the future for the* *common good.*[85]

> A time to stop and reflect is critical for all of us to learn from our own experiences and to learn together from the combined wisdom of the community.

Talking about important things

In the fast-moving world in which we all live and work, it is difficult to find time to talk about things that matter. Peter Block captures this clearly in his book *The Answer to How Is Yes.*[86] He recognizes that we so easily allow our vision to slip down to what we do rather than wrestle with the loftier and difficult questions of Why? What is important? What matters? Who do you intend to be? One of the companies with which I work asks me to sit down with their top leadership team several times a year to focus on who they are, who they are becoming, and who they intend to be. They deliberately do not want to talk about what they are doing or what their business strategies should be. We build community by asking the important questions: Who am I? Where do I belong? What do I care about? What legacy am I leaving? What is the purpose of my life? Why am I here?

Listening, caring, mentoring

Telling our stories is useful as a tool for personal reflection. However, for it to become a team building strategy, others have to listen. Community building is about learning how to listen, about caring enough to take another's story seriously. In community we invite one another to take the role of mentor and ask us about our story, raising the questions that pull learning from the narrative in a way that others can build on it. Listening well may be the most important component of relationship building and community life.

Celebrating and weeping

Teams that work together as communities seek opportunities to celebrate achievement – both team success and individual accomplishment. Every celebration reinforces the shared vision, the development of team members and the value of each contribution. It's another chance to gather around food and reflect. However, just as teams celebrate success, they weep together over loss. As I write this page, the front page of the *Pasadena Star News* tells the story of an employee commuter van from the Jet Propulsion Laboratory that yesterday went off a mountain road, killing three and injuring seven. Employees interviewed on television wept openly, commenting that JPL is a community, a family. They celebrate every person's achievement as a corporate success. But now they weep together, mourning the loss of three colleagues as a deep corporate wound. Communities celebrate and weep over the joys and the sorrows of their members.

Carrying each other's loads

Teams back one another up. Community takes this a step further and picks up the other's load. "Bearing one another's burden" is the biblical inspiration. Building community means helping one another when needed. Over nine days in February we skied across the Sierra Nevada Mountains from Lee Vining to Yosemite Valley. We gave ourselves ample time to cover the 44-mile journey, following the snow covered road most of the way. During a layover day in Tuolumne Meadows, we left our packs in camp and skied off to explore the backcountry. On one ill-considered run down a slope, I crashed wildly at the bottom. While falling was not unusual, this time I twisted my back and found myself with significant pain. Putting on the 60+ pound winter pack the next day was almost impossible. Don, however, stepped in and took much of my load onto his pack for the next day. With reduced weight I could ski reasonably well and after another night's rest I could carry my full pack. This was community in action. Don, recognizing my need, took on my load until I could carry it myself. It has also become part of our history and evolution. Because Don complained so much about the excess clothing that I was carrying – that he now had to carry – we have all significantly reduced our personal supplies and try to limit our packs to under 30 pounds in summer and under 40 pounds in winter.

Confronting accountability

Community, however, does not carry someone's burden when they could and should be doing it themselves. Building community is not an excuse for irresponsibility. In fact, we would argue that community requires accountability. The community expects everyone to belong and to contribute so that needs are met and objectives attained. A strong community cares enough for its members to hold them accountable to their commitments and to confront them when necessary. Confrontation is a sign of caring. I distinguish between confrontation and criticism. Confrontation is holding you accountable for your stated values and commitments because I care about you. Criticism is often holding you accountable to my stated values and expectations because I care about me. Communities care enough to confront their members and expect accountability.

Nurturing the shared vision

This, of course, is the heart of building community. The team community exists because of the shared vision of the team. Community is built when we work together to accomplish something beyond ourselves. Community develops when we understand that we could not do this alone, that we need others and that they depend upon us to realize the shared vision. Leaders have the assignment to keep the vision before the team. But communities reinforce the links that bind them together when every member takes the vision to heart and holds it before the team.

Remembering

Communities form around shared vision and together they create shared values. They maintain their momentum by cherishing shared memories. Remembering is a significant component of community building. We do it all the time on our wilderness trips. Reminiscing rekindles the passions, the emotions and the relationships that have formed over the years. It reviews accomplishments upon which we can build and mistakes from which we can learn. It reminds us who we are and why we do this and it always retrieves something from the past that makes us laugh. In the next chapter I want to look at shared memory and the culture that teams create together. And then in Chapter 8 we will focus on the luxurious freedom of laughter and the humble perspective that humor promotes. Community helps teams remember. We build community by reflecting on where we have been and what we have accomplished together.

Communities stay connected

Teams are relational communities. Ideally a team will be located together where relationships are nurtured in everyday interactions. For our rope team, however, that cannot be. We are scattered across the United States and spend the majority of our lives in other communities: family, work, church, and friends. Only when we gather at the trailhead do we become a rope team. But we nurture the community side continually.

Even though we live in different cities, three of us meet for lunch every Thursday. Around another meal we talk, reminisce, and plan. Most of our trips now are initiated at this lunch. Several times each week emails fly back and forth among team members as we keep up with one another's lives, travels, celebrations, and sorrows. And often we talk by phone, following up on issues raised by trip or email. We care about each other and take the time to attend to what is going on in each other's lives. And we keep talking and eating and planning the next thirty years.

Questions for reflection

- With whom do you share meals?

- Where do you belong? Where will you be missed?

- What is important to you in life? What do you care about? What matters?

- Who are you? Who do you intend to be?

- What is the purpose of your life? What legacy are you leaving?

- Why are you a team? What vision unites you?

- How does your team build community?

- With whom are you sharing your story?

- What role does reflection play in your learning?

- How can you become a better listener?

- What gives you joy?

- What makes you weep?

Chapter 7

Not another picture!

Team memory creates and reinforces culture

Photo op

It really was a spectacular view. The third day of our climb on Mt. Rainier was beautiful. You could see for miles. Mt. Adams, Mt. St. Helens, Mt. Hood loomed on the southern horizon with Mt. Olympus off to the west. Everywhere we looked was awesome – when we took the time to look. Most of the time we focused on the route before us, watching where we put our feet. We were on the glacier now. Crevasses split the ice in long deep gashes running every direction. Picking a path with a maze of cold canyons under foot demanded our attention. The lead on each rope team chose a solid route between crevasses, occasionally easing gingerly over a snow bridge crossing a gaping space that disappeared down into the ice. Everyone on the rope had to pay attention. It was important to follow the person ahead and not wander off on an angle into a crevasse. When we stopped, we enjoyed the view; while we climbed we watched where we were going. It was a long day; we climbed for sixteen hours. Everyone was a little tense and tired.

Once again Brent hollered out, "Hey guys, could you stop a minute; I want to take a picture?" This drew a sharp response from Don: "Not another picture! Make it fast; I'm standing on a snow bridge!" Brent had stopped on a solid snow surface and saw a photo op framed in his photographer's brain. He needed this picture. When one person stops on a rope team, everyone stops. Usually we are tired enough to use Brent's photo opportunities as an excuse to rest. This time, however, when the rope stopped Don was crossing a snow bridge. We halted with him right in the middle. It looked thick enough to support his weight, but still not the kind of place you can relax and rest comfortably. We stopped briefly while Brent took the picture. Don didn't have the patience for Brent to take his usual second or third shot to be sure he got a good one. One click and we were off again. But when we reached the summit it was a different story. Now everyone wanted a picture. And we stood there freezing while Brent searched for the perfect angle, lighting, cloud patterns and took multiple shots. We did so willingly because Brent takes great pictures and we wanted a record of this achievement.

Brent has been our recorder of memories ever since he joined the team. He is a very accomplished photographer, with excellent equipment. Once we saw Brent's work, the rest of us left our cameras at home. It does mean that we can't complain as much as we feel like when he stops continually in search of the perfect picture. And he stops often. In the early days Brent carried a very high-end Hasselblad camera with various types of film, filters, and tripod. It seemed to take him considerable time to set up for each shot and the equipment was heavy. There was always some debate whether the camera equipment was group gear whose weight should be shared or personal gear that Brent chose to carry. Brent usually lost that debate. In recent years, Brent has retired the Hasselblad in favor of a high-end digital camera. This offers significant advantage. It is much lighter, takes great pictures, and takes a lot of pictures. Now after a trip, team members can expect a CD in the mail filled with a visual gallery of our completed trip, a wonderful memory of our team effort. New technology comes at a price, however. Digital cameras take hundreds of pictures and they can be continually erased until the perfect shot is captured. This camera has radically increased the number of stops we make to take another picture and, I'm sure, reduced the distance we can travel in a weekend. But we have memories.

Remembering is important

Memory lays the foundation for building the team and feeds the soul of the community. It fuels momentum, provides energy, and reinforces the team culture. Corporate memory allows us to review where we have been and what we have done. It recalls why we are on this journey, what we hope to accomplish. Remembering goes back to the beginning and connects the choices that bring us to the present. When we reminisce in the car on the way to a trail, we relive the events of the past three decades, we acknowledge the experiences that have accrued, the objectives that we have attained together, and we build confidence in our purpose together. We know from experience what we are capable of, what each person can contribute. Remembering builds on that experience.

Remembering also strengthens the relationships of community. As we retell the stories of trips past we revive the drama, the emotions, the fears, the laughter, the camaraderie that we shared. We remember together the dependency of the rope, the frustrations of failure, and the exhilaration of achievement. Human beings relate through stories;[87] we are emotional beings. Much of our interaction occurs at the intimate level of feeling. Stories recreate trips and rekindle the feelings we had as we shared the experience. They reinforce a sense of belonging as we "remember when *we...*" did something together. Corporate remembering is like participating again. It reminds us of our shared history, it celebrates our shared journey.

Memory creates momentum. And that can be positive or negative. Remembering failure can create fear, raise limitations, and lower expectations. But celebrating the accomplishments of the past empowers the present. Remembering what we did well together energizes a team; it raises expectations, creates anticipation. Reviewing the journey together keeps us moving forward in relationships, anticipating what we can yet accomplish, and, in some ways, planning the story that we will tell in the future. It is rare that any two members of our rope team spend much time together without remembering at least one event that we shared together. It reminds us of the importance of our relationships and how much we have learned together.

Remembering is a way of learning from the past

Teams that stay together for long periods of time develop a history together that reveals clearly how much has been learned over the years. Remembering is a way of learning from the past, modifying our behavior to avoid repeating mistakes. Much of our reminiscing is about the things we did wrong and how we adapted.

Our reflections on the past always start with "Little Jimmy." That was the first trip we took together and our ignorance was evident. We wore inadequate clothing and carried unnecessary and wrong equipment. We all remember how miserable we felt on that trip. It was that memory that enrolled us in the Sierra Club Basic Mountaineering Course and began a thirty year curriculum learning about wilderness travel. We now walk in snow-sealed leather boots or Gore-tex shoes with double layer wool socks. We learned about the wet-weather advantages of wool and then advanced to polypropylene and Polartec clothing. Ponchos were discarded immediately as we opted for full rain suits then migrated to Gore-tex breathable fabric to avoid over-heating when working in the rain. Now we wear ultra light-weight Precip raingear that keeps us dry and breathes in a heavy downpour. Memory makes a fast learner.

Our use of tents adapted more slowly. Early on we hiked into Onion Valley in the Sierra Nevada Mountains preparing to cross Kearsarge Pass into the backcountry of Kings Canyon National Park. The weather was good; our tents were light. After a full day of hiking and lunch on the pass, we crawled into our tents tired and ready for sleep. Don and I shared a two-person tent; Newt slept alone in an inexpensive tent with a pole in the center. Sometime after we had gone to sleep a storm arrived; it rained hard. We learned two things that night. First, we learned that inexpensive summer tents do not keep heavy rain out of the tent. Water slipped in and our sleeping bags got wet. Second, we learned that tents with poles in the center could collapse when you roll over in your sleep. This is a particular problem if it is raining hard and the tent is not waterproof. Water reached into both tents that night but when Don and I went to wake Newt in the morning we found a soggy orange mess of tent, pole, sleeping bag and Newt tangled together in a puddle of water. Remembering reminds us to choose appropriate equipment. We now have sturdy four-season tents for fall and winter camping that have withstood up to three feet of snow dumped on them overnight. We also have ultra lightweight three-pound silnylon spring and summer tents that sleep two or three persons comfortably. It was these silnylon tents that we carried on the 94-mile trek around Mt. Rainier this past September. We did have very heavy rain one night but part of the learning of thirty years is how to pitch the tent to prevent the water from coming in. I stayed quite dry and comfortable throughout the storm.

It only took one fall trip, hiking in warm sunshine with summer gear, to learn that fall can turn into winter overnight. One very long cold night was all it took for us to learn that summer gear in California works until September. After that the wise wilderness traveler goes prepared for winter. Memory keeps that in mind when we pack. And remembering together teaches new members what we have learned.

Remembering can also be held against you. Brent will never live down leaving the car keys locked in the trunk of a car 20 miles from the car we needed to drive. And the group checks the map whenever I suggest that a trip is basically level. We took a family trek one year – a twenty-mile point-to-point backpacking trip over a summer weekend. I chose a beautiful trail, appropriate for including the wives and children. I noted that it started and ended at about 3,500 feet of elevation and was "basically level." It was a trip Beverly and I had taken several times before with our two sons. I did not remember it as strenuous. Somehow my memory had flattened out the steep ups and downs over the ridges and passes and through the canyons and valleys. What I had called easy, the family team declared strenuous. Fortunately, the relationships were strong enough that my punishment, like Brent's, has only been to be reminded about my poor judgment for the past twenty years! I recently retraced this particular hike and noticed that it seemed to have become much steeper than I remembered.

We learn from the past. Remembering together keeps that learning fresh and equips us for the team decisions we face today. It's how we keep moving forward. Celebrating the past makes it possible for us to envision the future.[88]

Remembering is a way of reinforcing shared values

The exercise of corporate memory builds the team culture, reinforcing the ideals that have become important over the years. Remembering is storytelling; it is the way we pass on what we believe, what we value. Storytelling is also selective. We choose to retell the stories that communicate what we think is important. The team embeds its values and builds its culture around the stories it remembers. We talk about the rock vote at Mosquito Lake when the weather was deteriorating as the trip began. While we did not like the idea of rain all weekend, we were prepared and most members of the team voted 3–2 either to continue on or to leave. One new member however voted 5–0 to leave. That skewed the vote and we left. But the story emerges often in the team corporate memory as a way of reminding ourselves and others who join us that our decisions should take the team into account alongside of our personal preferences.

Similarly the story about changing socks when we arrive at camp is remembered, often lifting up the values of taking responsibility, listening to experience, learning and growing, and taking the team seriously. It is clear from our stories that being a team is an important value that we want every participant to embrace. The stories of our equipment failures and successes underline our commitment to be prepared. The dramas of storms blowing us off the mountains are retold as a commitment to safety and to future climbs together. In my work as a leadership consultant and mentor I often say that you can tell what an organization values by watching the behavior of its employees. Their actions will always reflect their perception of the organizational culture – what is truly valued – regardless of what formal company statements proclaim. I think the same principle holds here. If you want to understand the culture of a team – the values that shape its work together – listen to its stories. As the team remembers together, it builds an accepted corporate history and tradition which governs its present and future decisions. Remembering reinforces what we think is important. Corporate memory shapes corporate culture.

> If you want to understand the culture of a team, listen to its stories

Memory is elusive and selective

We remember selectively to reinforce what we believe, but it's probably also true that the culture of the team constrains what we choose to remember. We remember the stories that move us forward and affirm who we intend to be. But memory is also elusive. Individual memory is more fragile and fleeting than most of us want to admit. We believe that we remember quite clearly. This is where the benefits of corporate memory are evident. Together we can remember more accurately than any one of us can remember personally. If I did not believe this before, it has been made blindingly clear in the writing of this book. As I think back on the stories of our rope team in action, I can see the events of each trip visibly in my mind. However, as I passed the draft of each story around to the members of the team for review, they wondered what trip I was on. When we sit together and remember the days and the details of a trip, it is amazing the pieces that each person has left out in their own mental reconstruction of events. When I first drafted the story about the near mutiny at Virginia Lakes, I sent it around and heard back immediately that the emotional events I wanted to illustrate were accurate, but the chronology I had outlined was not. In fact, I had completely blanked out two days of the trip in my mind. As we sat down and remembered together, small details noted by someone else triggered new memories for me. I was quite surprised by the selectiveness of my memory and the gaps that had to be filled in by others. Memory is elusive. Remembering is slippery. Alone we live with a construction of reality formed by the particular perspectives or emotions that filtered our experience of the events. Together we can design a story of events that is much closer to reality as perceived by the team. Corporate memory is likely to be more accurate than individual memory, although group memory probably also shapes individual recollection to some extent. Remembering together at least defines a shared interpretation of the journey as the team moves into the future.

Reminiscing rekindles relational intimacy

Over the years we have noticed that reflecting together on the experiences we shared renews our relational commitment. We remember together the joys we celebrated and the difficulties we weathered. Shared celebration and shared adversity make connections that memory can refresh. Retelling the stories reminds us of our shared history and strengthens the relationships as we head again into the wilderness.

Celebrating Don's birthday in the "Tenaya Lake Hilton" has become one of the legends of our team. We were skiing across the Sierra range one very cold February. The night we spent at Lake Ellery, the temperature dropped well below zero. Digging through ice to reach the lake was impossible. We had to melt snow for water. Skiing over Tioga Pass we arrived at Tenaya Lake in the Yosemite high country on Don's birthday. It was cold and windy; we were tired and chilled, and we noticed frequent tracks of roaming bears. Yosemite bears do not always hibernate due to the food sources available from campers and hikers. When we reached Tenaya Lake, everything was under snow as it should be but the door on the restroom that served summer travelers was not locked. By digging out a few feet of snow we could open the door and found inside a wonderfully sheltered room, cleaned and sanitized for the winter closure. Luxury! With wind and snow blowing outside and bears scrounging for food, we sat in relative warmth and secure comfort within the walls of the concrete bathroom. Spreading out our sleeping bags, we cooked dinner indoors and, shining our headlamps on the chocolate chip cookies we carried for dessert, we sang happy birthday to Don. For winter camping this was a five-star accommodation. It may well be the most memorable birthday that Don will ever have and surely the only one spent sleeping in the men's restroom at Tenaya Lake. Dubbed the Tenaya Lake Hilton, this story has been told and retold as a unique experience shared by members of the team.

Recognizing the importance of celebrating shared accomplishments the team will intentionally build in a time for reminiscing and crafting the story. After a night on the summit of Mt. Rainier the team descended to Seattle

> Reminiscing reinforces relationships

and gathered with spouses at the Salmon House to share a good meal and recall the details of our five days on the mountain. Consequently twenty-five years later when we completed the 94-mile trek around Mt. Rainier, we drove to Seattle and celebrated over a salmon dinner. Shared accomplishment creates memories; reminiscing reinforces relationships.

It may be even truer with shared adversity. Don, Brent, and I have a framed photo on our office walls that looks like a mountain on fire. It's Brent's recorded memory of Mt. Adams. We climbed Mt. Adams on a weekend outing. Starting late on a Friday afternoon we climbed slowly to a base camp from which we would climb to the summit on Saturday. Before we could set up the tents a windstorm whipped up. Violent, gusting winds ripped through our camp and clouds raced across the sky as sunset turned the horizon brilliant red. Brent's picture captures the flame-red clouds swirling around the mountain. It reminds us of a very uncomfortable night. The wind was much too strong to set up our tents. We cooked quickly huddling around the stove to protect it and still had dirt and debris in our food. We hollowed out space on the ground and climbed into our sleeping bags pulling the hoods tightly over our heads. It was a strange night. The wind was so strong it lifted the foot of our bags as it barreled through the camp. We didn't get much sleep. In the morning the wind had abated but the storm was gathering. Our sleeping bags and hair were filled with dirt and dust. The few tents that had been pitched by others were rags. And the storm was building. It did not take a rock vote to determine our plan. We retreated and descended to the car. To this day we have yet to reach the summit of Mt. Adams, but the photo reminds us daily of the power of a wilderness storm and the experience that Don, Brent, and I shared.

Everyone on the team remembers Glen Aulin. When we enter the Yosemite backcountry, we have to deal with bears. They have learned well how to feed off of backpackers. It is now a serious enough problem that we are required to carry bear canisters for our food. The bears are too smart for the hanging systems used elsewhere. Five of us trekked from Tuolumne Meadows to Glen Aulin to May Lake and Mt. Hoffman. The night at Glen Aulin was memorable. We set up camp as usual, enjoyed our dinner together, and sealed our food in the canisters for the night. But that didn't stop the bears. In the middle of the night, we woke to angry growling, clawing, and banging noises. The bears had found our canisters and were not happy. They knew that food was inside and they were biting, clawing, and knocking the canisters around the camp. When bears are angry the thin nylon walls of a tent give false comfort. We lay there awhile listening and finally generated enough group courage for all of us to get up and chase the bears off. I think we all slept lightly the rest of the night. The next morning we passed two other men who had camped near by without bear canisters. We gave them some granola bars to replace their breakfast.

Shared anxiety is a bonding experience. So is shared inconvenience. We have many more stories of travel mishaps beyond the misplaced keys. We laugh at Don's Volkswagen van that was so old and slow we could walk up Sherman grade faster. We marvel at the Bishop mechanic who found the part needed for Newt's antique International Harvester van and repaired it while we camped at the local hotel. We have not returned to Mineral King since I blew out my brakes and radiator on one trip. And of course there is much humor and reminiscing about my winter driving. As the only native Southern Californian on the team, I am no longer allowed to drive on winter trips. Three times we had to be towed out of snow banks when I was behind the wheel. It was a humiliating experience for those from back east. But the group bonded at my expense and I don't have to drive.

Remembering makes connections and reveals growth

Remembering together helps a team see how far it has come. When we look at the competence and the confidence we have today compared to our first trip together we can only celebrate our growth. That is one of the benefits of reminiscing. It shows the pattern of growth and encourages continued learning.

> We also recognize that a team with strong relational connections holds members secure on the rope while they pass through transition stages in other areas of life.

Rich, a professor of psychology on our team, notes that the research of Kenneth Pargament on coping strategies shows that a sense of personal efficacy and the social support of caring relationships give us tools for dealing with the larger issues of life. Being good at something like climbing a mountain and having a network of relationship in which to talk through concerns provides effective resources for coping with the natural stresses of life.[89] I remember well a deep conversation about love with Rich on Mt. Baldy. He was the only single man left on our team and was contemplating marriage. We remember discussing the pain of divorce hiking over Duck and Mammoth Passes, the murder of a brother as we soaked in the hot springs after climbing Black Mountain, the death of a parent while we skied into Rock Creek Lake, job changes as we trekked through Thousand Island Lakes, the birth of a grandson as we hiked in the backcountry of Zion National Park, and issues of retirement skiing across Lake Sabrina. Life is a journey through its own wilderness. Roped together to climb a mountain we help one another deal with the larger issues of life.[90] Together we reflect on change, loss, learning, growth, and who we intend to be. Remembering makes the connections between our corporate climbing together and our personal journeys through life. In some ways participation on the rope team provides the same security for living as it does for climbing. Someone will be there to hold you secure if you stumble and stay with you until you regain your footing. Strong relational teams can be resources for life.

Remembering challenges continued growth

Reminiscing by itself is not enough. We find a certain irony in the beginning of our climbing team. Three of us were in graduate school together but we didn't know each other. Another student announced the formation of a backpacking club and the three of us attended the initial meeting. We walked out of the meeting together, lamenting the limited vision of the club, which wanted to meet monthly and reminisce over slides of trips members had taken in the past. We did not mind reflecting on the past, but we wanted to explore the wilderness now. Talking together we found a kindred spirit and standing there in the hallway decided to take a trip together. That was the Little Jimmy experience and launched thirty years of mountaineering and relational growth.

Looking back, we still count the number of nights we spend in the wilderness. One year we reached fifty. That goal beckons us in the future. As we dispersed geographically around North America, the trips decreased in frequency. But every time we gather to remember together, we are encouraged to add another trip the next year. We may never get back to eleven trips per year, but we will keep growing together. Reflecting on our accumulation of equipment over the years does not stop us from buying more gear. In fact, as we consider increasing the trips as we get older we are looking for ways to decrease the weight that we carry. Researching, testing, and buying new ultra-lightweight mountaineering equipment fuels our desire to return to the mountains and the team ropes up for another trip.

Over the three decades, we have looked back often, remembering with fondness the successes and the fiascos of our team efforts. But that memory always serves a larger purpose: to motivate us to take another trip. Reflecting on the past helps us to envision the future.[91] It grounds our hope in history but lifts our eyes to the horizon. We want to keep climbing and we want to do it together. We are a team connected by vision, by relationships, and by thirty years of shared history.

Remembering

So how does a team cultivate the memories that strengthen its relationships, establish its culture, and encourage its future? We have been very intentional about this process. For the first six years, when we took a wilderness trip every month, we would gather between trips, reminisce, and plan the next trip. When we moved into the computer era, Don began printing a simple newsletter after each trip with a story by Dwyer and pictures of the trip. This too fueled our interest and was something we could share with our families. When Brent emerged as the designated photographer of trips, we looked to him to print and have framed an 11 × 14 photo to commemorate each trip. Most of us have several in our offices and homes, remembering the journeys that we took each year. Now in the age of CD and DVD, we expect a full travelogue of pictures following each trip and members of the team are building libraries of photos celebrating our accomplishments. And we continue to talk, have meals together, reminisce about trips past and anticipate trips coming. Don, Dwyer and I have lunch every Thursday. Brent, Newt, Rich, and Steve are regularly connected by email or telephone. Because we are a team, most of us have our email set up as a list. Any memo to any member of the team, regardless of its subject matter, tends to be distributed to the entire team. In fact, if someone is left off they feel left out. Being a team is about more than the specific objective ahead. It is about sharing life. We are roped together.

Remembering is an important component of team cohesiveness. Over time the selection and retelling of stories forms a culture, a way of being together and that culture shapes the team we are becoming and the stories we will tell. Every photo Brent takes celebrates yesterday and envisions tomorrow. Remembering keeps the team's vision alive; it keeps the shared values clear. Remembering energizes our continued participation and rekindles the relationships of community. Remembering keeps our future roped to our past and it keeps us all tied into the rope. And it keeps us laughing together.

Questions for reflection

- What do you remember?

- What stories do you tell most often?

- What have you learned lately?

- What events or choices have brought you to this place in life?

- With whom do you reminisce? What do you talk about?

- What are the benchmarks of your team's history? What memorable experiences are recounted?

- Who listens to your stories? Who shares your journey?

Chapter 8

"Boy do I have gas!"

Teams allow humor to keeps things in perspective

It was our annual October trip. This time we planned to climb one of the Three Sisters Mountains in Central Oregon. We all flew into Portland, rented cars, and drove to Bend. From Bend, we headed up the Cascade Lakes Loop toward the Sisters' trailhead and right into a blizzard. The road was closed for winter many miles from the start of the trail. And of course this time we did not have skis. So we returned to Bend and decided to explore Smith Rocks as our annual adventure. Along the way we stopped at a small market. Now it should be noted that increased elevation often causes some uncomfortable gastric responses from our internal organs. As we got out of the car Don experienced a moment of such discomfort. Walking to the market entrance he pulled the door open, commenting audibly back over his shoulder: "Boy do I have gas!" and turned to face two young women coming out the door. They enjoyed the humor of the moment as Don's face blended well with his red hair. As he stood there

> Humor is an additive that fuels team spirit

embarrassed, holding the door open for the women, the rest of us could hardly stand up we were laughing so hard. Don will never hear the end of that remark. Humor is an additive that fuels team spirit.[92]

Remembering relives the humorous moments

The story of Don's embarrassing comment has been retold often in the car on the way to a trailhead, over meals together, and on the trail. It is one of many stories over which we reminisce, mining once again the humor of the moment and reclaiming the laughter that frees our spirits. Laughter is wonderful. It's refreshing and addictive. We banter and tell these stories intentionally, enjoying our time together because we know that effective teams like being together – they have fun together.[93] The telling of stories, the self-deprecating or humbling banter keeps us relaxed and relational. The accumulated stories of shared team experience provide a rich source of humor which we never tire of rehearsing.[94]

Humor is a strange thing – difficult to define. What is funny to one may not be to another. For some it means surprise or exaggeration; for others it emerges from disconnects or absurdities. Humor is often seen in stories that show our frailties and justify our imperfections. "Humor is a universal and essential social and cultural phenomenon. It is a vital part of the ways in which we understand and express ourselves on just about anything of importance in our lives."[95] Humor may be as ambiguous as memory, but like memory it thrives and finds expression at the intersection of relationships. Humor is integral to the life of successful teams.[96]

Humor remembers with laughter and learning

When a team learns together, its history accumulates anecdotes of errors, foolishness, and idiosyncrasies. This is where we find the most humor. We have no trouble acknowledging our frailties and laughing at the absurdities of our efforts.

Learning to use Nordic skis generated some of the most contagious laughter I can remember. We were all new to this sport. Some had done alpine skiing before, but no one had snapped their toes onto skinny skis, tried to climb slopes without slipping, and then descend with uncontrolled speed. We practiced together and we learned, and the process was humorous. Nordic skis are supposed to grip the snow as we climb to mountain passes. Occasionally they do. But just as often, skis slide out from under us leaving us face down in the snow. When we do reach the top, skiing down becomes the challenge. Nordic skis lock the toes but not the heels. Turning is an art – an art that some learned slowly and some never learned – which makes the fall an important technique to master. And this we became good at. We took some spectacular falls: head-over-heels falls; skis-flailing-in-the-air falls; head-on-collision falls with people, rocks, and trees. At one point, Rich lost control and flew into a snow bank head first so deeply that only his legs and skis were sticking out. It was hard to stop laughing long enough to pull him out. And his irritation that we were laughing only fueled our laughter more. I remember coming home that day with aching ribs, less from the falls I took than the depth of the laughter that had consumed me. We laughed hard while learning and continue to enjoy the humor in retelling the stories.

Our introduction to canoeing was similar, and we remember the stories with great enjoyment. Don is the river enthusiast on our team. He had canoed rivers in the east and convinced me to join him for a three-day trip on a 30-mile stretch of the East Carson River running from central California into Nevada. He organized the equipment, planned the route, checked the water level, and basically did everything. I came along for the ride. As we packed the canoe along the river's edge, I commented that the water seemed to be moving rather fast. Don assured me that it would be no problem controlling the open canoe in this river. And besides, he noted, he had brought along the definitive book on canoeing as well as a river map that explained what we would be encountering. If we ran into any difficult problems we could stop and consult the book and map.

Somewhat calmed, I climbed into the front of the canoe and was immediately alarmed again by the precariousness of my perch and the seeming instability of the canoe even while we floated in calm water near the shore. About this time, a high mountain glacier with crevasses was sounding quite stable and secure compared to this swirling water. Again he spoke words of reassurance and we cast off into the river. Immediately we were caught up in the current and swept downstream with icy water splashing into my lap with each bouncing wave. Don yelled at me to paddle to the left. I was worrying about staying in the canoe. He could paddle!

Swiftly the current rushed us downstream but with each minute we were gaining confidence and some semblance of control – at least for the first seven minutes. Then we rounded the bend, got caught in an especially fast current and were being swept straight into a huge rock face stretching across half the river. Desperately we paddled, furiously attempting to get the canoe out of the current's pull and angled away from the rock face. But no such luck. We crashed head on into the rock face, swamped the canoe, rolled it over on top of us, dumped our poorly tied camping equipment into the river, and soon found ourselves bobbing down the rushing river like corks held up only by our life vests.

I didn't think I would drown but as I watched our canoe and all my gear speeding downstream, I had visions of a very wet, very hungry, very long 30-mile walk to where our car was waiting for us. With the help of panic and the current we scrambled to shore and discovered that God continues to watch over fools. A kayaker downstream had collected our canoe and all of our gear and pulled to shore to wait for us. Our 30-mile walk was only 300 yards.

While Don tied the equipment in securely this time I read the little map that explained the river. And what did I read? At the ten minute mark was a big warning, in capital letters: "WATCH OUT FOR THE SLAMMER! Canoeists are advised to walk their canoe around this bend to avoid a major rock face overhanging the river." Now we find out!

With considerably less bravado, we coaxed our canoe down the river for several miles and found a flat sunny area where we stopped early. The rest of the afternoon was spent drying out food, tent, sleeping bags, and clothing, none of which had stayed dry in our waterproof canoe bags. We also pulled out the definitive book on white-water river canoeing, dried each page and proceeded to read about life in a canoe on a western white-water river, particularly the chapter on disasters. It's never too late to learn. With the knowledge we were able to derive from this time of study and humble reflection, we negotiated the remaining miles of the river over the next two days and finished the trip exhilarated by the experience and the new level of skills we had obtained.

So we built on this experience. Brent and Steve became a second canoe team. Dwyer bought a kayak, probably so he did not have to experience the conflict of paddling with a partner. Each year we improved. We read books on canoeing, watched videos, and we practiced. We studied rapids before we entered them and learned how to plan a strategy that would see us through without capsizing.

On our third trip to the Trinity River in northern California, we were in the middle of a 40-mile stretch of river and had come to a cascading rapid that we had walked around in previous years. We stood on a cliff above the rapids and studied the river. The river dropped through a roiling cascade about 200 feet directly toward a wall of rock. As the water rushed against the rock, it surged backwards pushing the current sharply to the left downstream and around another bend. We thought we had learned enough to try it. We planned our strategy and returned to the river. Placing the bow of the canoe into the top of the cascade we plunged down toward the rock wall, Don steering in the stern while I used a bracing stroke to keep the bow up out of the waves. Just as we touched the water surging back from the rock we executed a textbook perfect cross-draw stroke and turned neatly into the current rushing past the rock wall and floated comfortably down the river.

We were exhilarated. Everything we had learned and planned had worked flawlessly. All our study and practice had paid off. We knew how to do it. We cheered and rehearsed the perfection of our maneuver, relaxing as our adrenalin returned to normal, oblivious to the fact that we were still floating rapidly downstream.

Suddenly Don noticed two rocks directly in the middle of the river. Without time to plan we snapped to attention and steered between the rocks. I have vividly etched in my memory a pure green tongue of water that converged between those rocks as we slid out over a two-foot drop we had not seen. Don says my last words were "We don't do this!" as the bow of the canoe plunged down and I went flying over the front of the canoe into the cold river. But not for long. With a mixture of adrenalin and desperation I shot out of the water like a submarine fired missile and slid back into the canoe so fast Don was surprised.

The Slammer and the Green Tongue have become part of the lore of our group. While we did not think things were humorous as we were dumped into the river, looking back at the stories always evokes laughter from all of us as we reflect on our foolishness and arrogance. Humor is appropriately humbling and puts things in perspective. It also is instructive. We cannot laugh at these stories without remembering to study the map before we start the trip and be prepared for what is around the next bend of our journey.

Humor relieves tension

Studies being conducted at the University of Michigan and the University of Maryland underline something most of us already know: laughter is about the most effective way there is to relieve tension. Humor creates a connection between people and reduces tension.[97]

In 1998 I joined Canadian Himalayan Expeditions for a trek to the Mount Everest Base camp. We were told at the beginning of the trip that the two weeks allotted for this trek would not be enough time for every person to acclimate to the altitude. Normally one-third of the trekkers are not able to adjust in this timeframe and become too sick to reach the base camp at 17,200 feet. Since none of us had been this high before, we did not know if we were going to be able to acclimate. A note of tension hung over the table as we would gather in the dining tent for meals. We talked about our aspirations and uncertainties. About the third day of the trek we were gathered for breakfast reflecting on the long steep trail ahead when the oldest trekker on our team came in with his wife. He was a medical doctor, a large outgoing man, with an infectious humor. This was his first camping trip ever. His wife had talked him into it. On this morning his anxiety emerged as irritability. He groused loudly at the table, "I don't know how the rest of you get your sleeping bags packed so quickly. I roll it up carefully and have a terrible time getting the stuff sack to fit around it." We looked up in surprise and laughed. I suggested that he try stuffing his bag in the stuff sack. Then we laughed even more that he had never thought of that. No one had taught him that we don't roll bags any more. We stuff them into their sacks and cinch them down tightly. That laughter relieved the tension in everyone's mind and the stuff sack became an item of trail conversation through the day. And the Sherpas were right; only four of us chose to go higher than 16,000 feet. Effective teams use humor and stories to relieve tension and relax relationships.[98]

Humor handles embarrassment

The same trek to Nepal showed me how humor also handles embarrassment. The Sherpa guides told us at the beginning of the trip that even though we were strangers we would find ourselves talking together about every bodily function before the trip was over. We were not sure but too embarrassed to pursue the matter. And they were right. Two weeks on the trail in intimate proximity with seven strangers sharing a toilet tent while stomach rumbling increases with each 1,000-foot of elevation gain is a formula for embarrassment. Most have stomach problems; many have diarrhea. And everyone knows it. At first this was awkward, embarrassing. But, as predicted, before long these natural bodily processes became the topic of conversation at every meal as we monitored each other's health and encouraged one another. And we laughed. We laughed at the unreality that we could be having these kinds of conversations with strangers, over meals no less. And the laughter handled our embarrassment, putting it in proper perspective. Once again the Sherpas were correct.

The challenge to dispose of human waste in the backcountry has long hounded wilderness travelers. Our team has faced this issue many times with its fair share of chagrin and embarrassment and considerable humor. Newt's experience, however, has become legend.

We were camping at Rock Creek Lake on a winter trip into the Sierras. We had skied from the point where the road was closed to a base camp carved out of the accumulating snow. We set up the tents and began to prepare dinner. Newt chose this time to take care of his bathroom needs and with shovel and toilet paper he skied off into the bushes. A short time later we heard a howl of protest as Newt roared with indignity. Newt had skied to a discrete location behind trees and bushes far from river and people. He had cleared out some space to complete his objective, stuck his ski poles in the snow, slid back a pace, squatted, went to the bathroom, cleaned up, pulled up his pants and reached for his poles. That is when he slipped. Skis shot forward and he sat down hard right in his own waste.

At the time Newt did not see the humor of the moment. The rest of us, however, were rolling in the snow doubled up with laughter. When he finally cleaned up, Newt also was able to join us in laughter. And once again laughter handled embarrassment and kept things in appropriate human perspective.

Humor allows us to acknowledge our fears and share them

Just as humor deals with tension and embarrassment, so it helps us manage fear. It creates a distance from potentially stressful situations so that we can deal with them more rationally.[99] We use humor and tell jokes as a way of helping us understand and work with something we fear.[100]

When we lay in the tents at Glen Aulin anticipating the visit of bears, we remembered Rich's experience in Little Yosemite Valley and laughed. The first night of his weekend trip, Rich set up camp and hung his food creatively high out of reach of any bear. But he underestimated the intelligence of Yosemite bears. In Yosemite, bears have trained their cubs to go out on the limb on which food has been hung. When they do, the limb breaks and cub and food fall to the ground. Dinner is served. In the morning, hungry and with nothing but a shredded food bag, Rich hiked out to the valley in search of a meal. It was a short weekend. We laughed and slept and awoke to our own bears. But we had breakfast in the morning.

Laughter seems to balance single issue focus

One of the wonders of wilderness travel is singleness of focus. Most of us live busy lives, constantly surrounded by demands on our time, claims on our attention, issues needing resolution. Seldom do we have the luxury of dealing with one thing at a time. We are multi-tasking people with professional careers. In the wilderness, however, priorities change. Survival tunes the mind and focuses the attention. The basic demands of life dominate our thinking: eating, sleeping, shelter, and health replace life's normal diverse agendas. The destination of the trip is the only objective we have to worry about. For busy people, this intimate focus is refreshing and liberating. I am not surprised that I laugh more in the wilderness than in any other context of life. With the intensity of a single all-consuming experience or purpose, a team finds itself connected and united in what Mihaly Csikszentmihalyi calls "flow." And when we are in this space together, we banter and joke and laugh easily. Humor and joy are natural expressions of contented intensity.[101]

One May we were exploring the backcountry west of Bishop. As we wandered up a canyon we had to cross a river flowing full with spring run off. It took us some time to carefully pick our way across, balancing precariously as we stepped cautiously from rock to rock. When we all reached the other side, we continued up the canyon. That was when the earthquake hit. The ground shook. The trees swayed. It sounded like a train roaring down the canyon. The south wall of the canyon began to avalanche. Down the north wall, large boulders bounced to the valley floor. Once we realized what was happening, we reversed our direction and took off at a run toward camp. The river that had detained us for nearly thirty minutes was crossed in about thirty seconds. We wanted out of that canyon. Back at camp, as our adrenalin dropped, we could only laugh. The speed and accuracy with which we crossed the river the second time was awesome. One thought propelled us and now that we were safe our behavior was laughable. This mixture of focus and humor is addictive. We enjoy our time together and we keep coming back.

Laughter is a measure of the health of the team

Effective teams measure their health by the relaxed humor and banter that exists. Laughter may be a good barometer of team condition. Research suggests that laughter is good for us. Laughter is an integral part of wellness; it oxygenates the blood, relaxes the muscles, and works out major internal systems.[102] A study described in *The Scientist* seeks to demonstrate that laughter not only changes mood and reduces stress, but also influences the body's pain control system.[103] Teams need relaxed relationships. Humor flows from that relaxed environment and contributes to it. We laugh so hard in the mountains that our ribs ache and our eyes weep. That kind of uncontrolled laughter clears the mind and cleans the lungs. It has to be healthy. And when we laugh together, it leads to cohesion and bonding among team members. Don was the one embarrassed in front of the market, but we all shared his embarrassment and we all saw the humor in the moment. We didn't laugh at him, we laughed with him and that laughter continues to this day.

When we relax and have fun we see humor in everything. Mood is contagious. If we are in a good mood everything is funny; when we are in a bad mood, nothing is. A negative mood seeks negative and serious things and negativity reinforces itself.

> So fun seems superficial, humor seems a waste of time, and people who aren't equally serious are dispensable. Too bad, because part of what makes a family [team] close is being able to enjoy each other. Being able to play and joke and laugh and act silly and do entertaining things together that *don't* require an existential analysis is some of the strongest glue that can hold a family [team] together.[104]

If a team is not having fun together, it probably is not doing its best.[105] On our climbing and canoeing teams we have fun. We work hard, but we enjoy what we do and we enjoy each other. We deal with the serious issues of life and death, but we also laugh at our personal pathologies and idiosyncrasies. We laugh at Brent's impeccable outfits and Newt's eclectic mismatched mosaic of clothing. We laugh when Steve's Frisbee breaks during a game because the temperature has dropped below freezing.

And we laugh when Newt thinks he is saving weight by using a Frisbee for a dinner plate. We laugh when my snoring drives Dwyer to his own tent, requires everyone else to cover their heads, and earns me many shoves in the night. We laugh at the coincidence that whenever a career decision has to be made a bird dumps on Don's head. We laugh at the stupidity of trying to ski across a snow-covered log crossing a river. We laugh at the rented canoe wrapped around rocks in Weitchpec Falls and how much some local men charged us to rescue Brent's camera equipment from the canoe. We laugh at Don, the purist, who was the last to give up snowshoes, the last to stop waxing skis, the first to weigh everything he carries on a postal scale and the one who just cut the floor out of his tent to sew in lighter material. We laugh at Newt, the only person I know who has been locked in the toilet stall of a ranger station and the only person I have found standing on a mountaintop singing hymns of the Methodist Church to the moon at the top of his lungs. We laugh a lot. On a rope team everything is focused, but regularly balanced with fun and laughter.

Humor keeps everything in perspective

Teams use humor to maintain perspective. We are driven by purpose and shared vision; we are constrained by our values, the culture of the team and the capability of its members. But the relationships that rope us together are nourished by the humor we embrace.

> The most successful team players we studied also skillfully mix substantive comments with a sense of humor in group interactions. They are counted on to offer the fresh perspective that no one else has considered. Most important, they try not to take themselves too seriously; the best team players also try to be self-effacing.[106]

Humor vents our emotions; it lowers our masks and allows us to work comfortably together as fallible, striving human beings. A serious intention brings the team together. We have a goal, an objective and we have an accepted way of doing things together.

But we have learned over the years that the success of our goal and the continuation of our team are directly related to the enjoyment we experience on the trail together. Humor creates just the right amount of slack in the rope so we enjoy the trip. And laughter is like a good rain. It clears the air and makes everything sharper to the eye. It allows us to enjoy each other and keeps us roped together.

Questions for reflection

- What makes you laugh?

- Where do you laugh? With whom do you laugh?

- What is the most absurd thing you have done recently?

- Who keeps humor alive in your team?

- Where do you preserve singleness of focus in your life?

- Using humor as the measure of health, how would you assess your team?

- How do you have fun?

- Who keeps you from taking yourself too seriously?

- How do you keeps things in perspective?

Chapter 9

Base camp

Teams embrace the whole person and family

The trek to the Mount Everest Base Camp was a trip that surrounded me with the awesome majesty of the Himalayas, even as it reminded me of the death that lurks in the thin air. When we left the village of Dugla and climbed toward Gorakshep below the base camp, we passed a memorial for one of the guides who died on a disastrous expedition two years earlier.

On May 10, 1996 eight climbers with the Adventure Consultants Expedition reached the top of Mt. Everest, which at 29,035 feet is the highest point on earth. Mike Groom, Rob Hall, Doug Hanson, Andy Harris, Jon Krakauer, Yasuko Namba, Ang Dorje Sherpa, and Norbu Sherpa stood on top of the world rejoicing in their achievement. The team had placed six climbers and two Sherpa guides on the summit. The story of this climb is one of the best known outside of climbing communities. Its triumphs and tragedies have been chronicled in books by Jon Krakauer, Anatoli Boukreev, Lene Gammelgaard, Sherry Ortner and Beck Weathers, made into a movie, *Into Thin Air,* and included in the IMAX documentary *Everest*.[107]

Rob Hall was co-founder with Gary Ball of Adventure Consultants, a New Zealand based guide service for expeditions and treks. Adventure Consultants have led a record-setting seventy-three ascents of Mt. Everest, taking climbers from twelve countries to the summit. The 1996 climb was the fifth time Rob Hall reached the summit of Mt. Everest. It was also his last.[108] The 1996 Adventure Consultants expedition was put together to lead

eight climbers to the summit of Everest. The expedition
consisted of twenty-six guides, climbing Sherpas, doctors, base
camp managers, cooks, and sirdars, supervising numerous
porters and yak herders. And that is just the group that arrived at
base camp nearly 12,000 feet below the summit of the mountain.[109] Behind such an expedition stands a very large network of
financial backers, suppliers, media relationships, and the organization of Adventure Consultants. In addition to the organizing
efforts of Adventure Consultants, every climber brought to the
expedition a personal support system that encouraged him or
her and made it possible. It takes a lot of people to put a rope
team on the summit of Mt. Everest.

Base camp is operational headquarters for a climbing expedition. Base camp is home. It is the local restaurant, the local hospital, and the communications link to the rest of the world. All of the
support systems necessary to sustain a summit attempt are
centered at base camp. From base camp supplies are ferried up to
four high camps en route to the summit. Climbers move up and
down between high camps, acclimatizing to the elevation and
conserving their strength for the final push to the summit. From
the last high camp to the summit there is no longer time to restore
a climber's strength. After 25,000 feet, the body begins to die, not
to rest. The final climb from high camp to the summit and back is
one shot and then a person needs to descend and recuperate.

On the memorable ascent of May 10, 1996, eight climbers,
three guides and two Sherpas from Adventure Consultants
headed for the summit. Other expeditions were on the mountain
as well. At one point that morning thirty-three climbers were
attempting to ascend the summit ridge, crowding the route. Beck
Weathers, a pathologist from Dallas, discovered to his surprise
and great disappointment that the high altitude caused his recent
cornea surgery to interfere with his sight. His cornea flattened
and he basically lost his ability to see. He had to turn back
without reaching the summit. Rob Hall, the team leader,
instructed Weathers to stay where he was until Hall could
summit and return with Doug Hanson to lead Weathers back to
the high camp. Beck Weathers waited; Hall and Hanson did not
return. A storm struck and Weathers started to freeze. From that
point on the situation seemed to spiral out of control. Doug

Hanson collapsed on the descent from the summit. Rob Hall stayed with him and they both died on the mountain. Andy Harris tried to go to their rescue and was lost on the mountain. Yasuko Namba also ran out of strength after reaching the summit. Both Namba and Weathers were found by climbers from another expedition who went for help. However, since Namba and Weathers were deteriorating so fast, they were left for dead on the mountain. At that high elevation you have to be able to save yourself. No one else has the strength or energy to do it for you. Yasuko Namba died, having been the second Japanese woman to reach the summit thereby completing her personal goal of climbing the highest mountains on the seven continents. Beck Weathers should have died. Driven by a powerful epiphany of his wife and children, he stood up and struggled down, miraculously finding high camp IV. Through wide-ranging relational connections, political intervention, government resources, and heroic efforts, he was picked off the mountain by helicopter and returned to Dallas and after several years of surgery and reconstruction has returned to his medical practice with a very different outlook on life and relationships. His story is retold poignantly and revealingly in his book *Left for Dead: My Journey Home from Everest.*[110]

This expedition climbed Mt. Everest because a large network of relationships and resources made it possible for the necessary people and supplies to be at base camp. And base camp supported the climbers. It was also true, however, that every person on the climbing team was there with diverse motivations, emotional attachments, and a personal network of relationships and resources making his or her participation possible. No one ties on to a rope team as an isolated individual. "It is impossible to remove the individual completely from layers of social relationships – family, organizational, institutional, community, societal, cultural. The individual carries these systems along in coping and these systems may assist in the coping process or create obstacles and impediments of their own."[111] The team exists because of its support system, and every member joins the team shaped by a personal history of life and relationships. The information published about Rob Hall and Beck Weathers illustrates well this reality.

Rob Hall was thirty-five years old – one of the most experienced mountaineers on Everest that day. This was his fifth trip to
the summit. He founded his company with his friend and partner
Gary Ball, and was recognized for his ability to help client
climbers reach the summit. He was also known for his strict
guidelines when safety was involved. He took people to the
summit, but he brought them back alive. Hall's wife Jan understood his passion and supported his work even though she recognized the risk it entailed. At the time of this climb Jan was
pregnant. Most of the books written about this expedition talk
about Rob Hall's effort to help Doug Hanson reach the summit.
Hanson had tried to climb Everest with Hall before, but ran out
of strength and had to turn back before reaching the summit.
This time he wanted to reach the top and Hall was committed to
get him there. They had to break one of Hall's safety rules about
turn-around time to make it, but Hall did lead Hanson to the
summit. On the descent, however, Hanson collapsed and Hall
found himself stranded too high with a failing climber and a
blind Weathers waiting for him below with no other guides to
assist him. Beck Weathers recounts the poignant conversation
between Rob and Jan as Hall sat dying on the mountain.

Rob lived through that night, but late the next afternoon, as darkness
began to fall, when there was no longer any hope of a rescue, Base
Camp called his wife, Jan, in New Zealand and patched her through to
her dying husband. Everyone on that mountain with a radio bore silent
witness to their last moments together. Hall had regained his facul-
ties. He and Jan decided at that moment to name their unborn child
Sarah.

Jan to Rob: "Don't feel that you're alone. I'm sending all my positive
energy your way."
Rob to Jan: "I love you. Sleep well, my sweetheart. Please don't worry
too much."

Both of them knew exactly what lay ahead. When those moments
had passed and Rob no longer had to be strong, you could hear him
quietly weeping, as he faced his own death. He didn't know the radio
was still on.[112]

Beck Weathers himself is a different story. A competent pathologist in Dallas, married with two children, Weathers suffered from deep bouts of depression. He found neither family nor work fulfilling. His friends feared he might be suicidal. His personal search for meaning and purpose led him to mountaineering. It became a passion, some would say obsession. He threw himself into climbs, developed his strength and abilities, and joined expeditions around the world. He did so without the support of his family. His wife Peach felt abandoned; his children never found him at home and when he was, he was depressed or preoccupied. Only his mountaineering lifted his spirits ... and took him away from home. Family vacations stopped because Weathers would rather be climbing. And when he was away he would not call or communicate for weeks at a time. By the time he decided to join the Everest expedition his wife had decided to leave him. She intended to tell him the marriage was over when he returned. But Mt. Everest changed his life in many ways. He lost one hand, the fingers on the other and spent months in the hospital with reconstructive surgery on his limbs and face. He was able to return to work as a pathologist with limited use of his hand. On the mountain, however, Weathers had an epiphany. He saw his family before him and decided clearly that that was the heart of his life, his reason for living. Looking back he reflected: "If you're going to come through an ordeal such as mine, you need an anchor. It may be your friends. It may be your colleagues. It may be your God. Or it may be, as it is for me, my family."[113]

That epiphany inspired him to get up and save himself when he should have died. Returning to Dallas, he redefined his priorities, asked his family to give him a second chance, and set out to regain their trust and love. When asked if he knew what would happen on Everest would he do it again he responded: "Even if I knew exactly everything that was going to happen to me on Mount Everest, I would do it again. That day on the mountain I traded my hands for my family and for my future. It is a bargain I readily accept."[114] He did not realize how much he needed his personal base camp until he returned from near death.

Eleven people died on Everest that May. Eight people from Adventure Consultants reached the summit. Four of them died.

If the objective were only to reach the top of the world, the expedition would have been a success. But the goal of a mountain climbing expedition, like the journey of life, is to return home. Summits are specific objectives on the journey but the descent to continue life is part of the goal of every climb. Summits come and go. This expedition is remembered for its notoriety, its successes, its failures, its drama, and its death. But each person on that expedition was a story of a life being lived for better or worse, individual stories with their own cast of characters, their own plot now interwoven into the team that ropes together for one leg of a journey shared together.

Life is an expedition

The metaphor of the rope tying leaders and followers together as a team working to achieve a shared goal is enriched by the concept of expedition. An expedition is a self-created group of people who organize to climb a mountain. It is usually a major undertaking. Funds have to be obtained, climbers recruited, equipment and supplies acquired, permits secured, and then dozens, often hundreds, of Sherpas and porters are hired to transport everything and establish a base camp from which the expedition will support the climb.[115] Climbing teams rope together to navigate a route up the mountain, advancing equipment and supplies into progressively higher camps from which other teams will move up the mountain. Everyone contributes to setting in place a final high camp from which those who are strong enough can attempt to summit. Often, as was the case on Annapurna, only one team reaches the summit to achieve the expedition's goal. Backup teams and everyone else on the expedition contribute so that the chosen team can attain the expedition objective. Frequently the expedition leader remains in base camp, managing the movement of climbers and supplies. When the lead team summits, the expedition succeeds with that particular objective.

On the 1996 Everest climb the expedition objective was not only for the expedition to summit, but for all of the client climbers to reach the top of the world and return home safely.[116] The narrow objective of summiting – embracing the personal motivations of individual climbers – ultimately resulted in expedition failure. Four members did not return, several were seriously injured, and the team leader died sitting on the mountain caring for an exhausted climber. Some rope teams succeeded in reaching the summit, but the expedition failed.

Life is an expedition. We are all on a journey – a search for meaning and significance in life.[117] For portions of that journey we choose to rope up with others to accomplish specific objectives. We form teams to achieve desired outcomes. And all of us belong to more than one team, more than one community, which are part of the larger expedition that gives purpose to our lives. Our expedition is an interconnected network of teams and communities moving us toward a chosen end. And as in most expeditions, we have multiple responsibilities. Simultaneously we belong to numerous communities with intersecting loyalties and expectations. Team members belong to families, to paid and volunteer work settings, to churches and clubs, to recreational groups and professional associations. These memberships provide a network of relationships that shape who we are becoming and these relationships also are impacted by the commitments we make and the teams we decide to join. These relationships are important connections in our search for significance.[118] And relationships are reciprocal. To some extent we are defined by the relationships in which we choose to invest and that investment in others impacts their lives as well. The complete network of relationships that defines us is our expedition. The team to which we are roped at any given point on the journey is only one team in our expedition.

Teams are only as strong as the members

Teams need to recognize that all of their members belong to multiple communities. A team member is more than a body clipped to the rope. We observe physical condition and watch for contributed competence. But every person on the rope brings his strengths and weaknesses, shaped by the diverse network that defines his unique personal expedition. We are much more than the role we play on a particular team.

Max De Pree tells a wonderful story of a millwright at Herman Miller, a Fortune 500 furniture manufacturer. When the millwright died, Max's father visited the family. As he sat awkwardly in the home expressing his condolences, the widow asked if she could read some poetry. She read several beautiful poems from a bound volume. When she finished, Max's father commented on the elegant poetry and asked who wrote it. The widow replied that her husband, the millwright, was the poet. That story became part of the culture of Herman Miller over the years, helping people understand that there is much more to a person than what we see in a particular role. Was he a poet that worked at Herman Miller, or a millwright who wrote poetry?[119] There is a larger story around each person tied into our rope. And that larger narrative reads into the life of the team.

When our rope team reaches the summit of a California mountain and poses for pictures, the photo shows seven climbers proud of what they have accomplished. But it does not completely reveal the persons present. There is more to these people than their professional careers or particular participation on our team. It might be evident that Brent is a photographer, but not as obvious that Dwyer does elegant woodwork, that Don organizes a cold weather shelter for the homeless, that Newt plays oboe in a band and directs plays, that Steve is an active ski patroller, or that Rich leads Spanish speaking missions to Haiti. These passions shape the people with whom I share a rope and contribute to the strengths and weakness they bring to a climb.

And again, these roles are single facets of complex lives. Every person on the team is a story being written, shaped by the forces present in the communities we join on our journey. Each person is the product of these intersecting communities. We are who we are because of the events of our lives and our network of relationships.[120] What happens in any community to which we belong affects who we are and the strengths, weaknesses, fears, and confidence we bring to the team. And a team is only as strong as its members. The strengths and weaknesses that make up who we are at any moment, shaped by our interactions with a network of relationships, govern what we bring to the team. What is happening in the larger life of team members can impact their contribution and thus further or limit team success. A rope team can only move as fast as its slowest member. A team has a vested interest in the larger life of its members.

Team success is tied to its members' support networks

What happens to one of us touches everyone on the team. Harvard psychologist Daniel Goleman has noted that mood is contagious; it spreads through a group.[121] If passions or anxieties are increased in another area of a person's life, they may find expression during the intense focus of team activity. I don't want to rope myself to a depressed person with suicidal tendencies unless I am feeling very strong! Which means I need to know what is going on in the larger life of the people to whom I am roped. A person under stress in another community will bring that stress to the team. It is hard to focus on the objectives at hand if our child is in the hospital, our mother is dying, or we just had a serious fight with our spouse. Stress can deplete physical condition, and that matters to a climbing team. Enthusiasm for an all-consuming project at work or church can take time away from preparation for the team climb. The successes and failures of life energize or drain the inner resources that we bring to the team on any particular trip. This is true for all teams but the rope makes it concrete. The people on the rope are whole persons. Their complete lives shape their contribution to team success. That is why a good team cares about what its members care about. The more we can help one another with our larger journey through life, the stronger the team will be.

Family is the team's base camp

Climbing and canoeing together for thirty years we have walked with each other through many family passages of life – marriage, divorce, children, sickness, grandchildren, retirement, death. While all of the communities in which team members participate are important, we have learned that family has the greatest impact on our time together. A mountaineering team depends upon a healthy family system. The family is base camp. It sends us out willingly or grudgingly and the team feels the difference. Given the amount of time we have spent in the wilderness over the years, we need the consent of our families to participate. And adding up all the money that we spend on equipment, supplies, and transportation we need the encouragement of the family. The time the team invests in trips is time away from spouses and children, from the responsibilities of home and family.[122] Without the support of our families, we would not continue. With the various persons who have participated on our team over the years, it is probably safe to say that the seven of us who are still active after thirty years are the ones whose families give us encouragement. Beverly has always recognized the value of the rope team for my personal growth and expression, and she has encouraged my participation enthusiastically. And it was not always easy for her. When our sons were younger, it was not convenient to care for them and keep an old house in order while she also worked and finished college. We both remember my son lamenting after a neighborhood shooting when I was off in the mountains, "Why does everything happen when Daddy's gone?" We know that our families pay a price to make our participation possible and we have worked hard over the years to keep them involved.

During the first six years when we took monthly trips into the California Sierras, one of us would host a family evening at our home between trips. Over dessert we would show slides of the last trip and tell the stories of our adventure, building enthusiasm for the next wilderness foray. These monthly family gatherings were always times of laughter as we recounted our follies, proclaimed our achievements and began to look at equipment catalogs for what we wished we had taken on the last trip. Beverly says that she could always gauge the success of the trip by how quickly I started talking about new gear.

We also scheduled family trips into the wilderness. We backpacked cross-country into the Cottonwood Lakes basin – Frisbee games, fishing, day climbs up Cirque Peak, shared meals, talking and laughter around camp. One of my sons fished all day while the other climbed the peak with Beverly, me, Debby, Rich, and Don. We camped at Joshua Tree National Park and practiced with ropes. Wives and children participated as well in rock climbing and rappelling. That was when I realized that children climb naturally without the fear that freezes me on the rock face. We hiked into Shadow Lake with side trips to Lake Edisa at the foot of Mt. Ritter. That was the trip my son caught trout with his bare hands. We were all impressed. We took the 20-mile "level" trek in Mt. Rainier National Park, pushing most family members to the limits of their comfort. We did winter ski trips in the Sierras. Not every family could participate every time, but over the years nearly every spouse and most children joined us for one or more family trips.

It has been especially gratifying to the team to see our children respond. My sons, Damon and Aaron, joined us on several trips, backpacking, skiing, rock and mountain climbing. Now that they are grown and married with children of their own, I am pleased to see their love of wilderness. Damon and Mary fish rivers from California to British Columbia, from Oregon to Colorado. Aaron and Monique have formed their own group of friends who take regular camping trips together. My four-year-old grandson Brendon is fascinated with the stories of mountaineering. He likes to tie into a rope and practice falling while I belay him. I have a picture on my desk taken of our rope team at a family barbeque last year. Six of the team are present along with Brendon who placed himself in the picture standing beside Steve. Matt Bosch has taken several trips with the team. He shared the bear encounter at Glen Aulin and climbed Mt. Hoffman. When the group pictures were distributed after Mt. Hoffman, Matt quite proudly identified himself as the "newest team member." David Stenberg participated in the 94-mile trek around Mt. Rainier this past September. It was a pleasure to spend ten days with David and benefit from his younger perspective on life and mountaineering. And David knows more about state-of-the-art mountaineering equipment than any of us. He is a human catalog of information and spurred us all on to update our gear … as if we needed encouragement. Matt and David have earned the right to participate as full team members on any of our future trips. Ashley Butman has picked up Rich's love of wilderness and works with him at Honeyrock Camp. And Stephanie Bosch has asked to go with us on a winter backcountry trip. It's wonderful to see the shared vision and shared values that have motivated us these past three decades finding expression in the next generation of our families.

The family is base camp. They support us in the objectives of the team, they encourage us to invest the time and money, and now they send new climbers for the rope. Last year Don hosted a barbeque at his home. Every member of the team except Rich was able to participate, along with spouses, seven of our children, and two grandsons. Without base camp we would not be an active team after thirty years. The family has been a critical support system for the team.

Good teams care about what their members care about

Because the team depends heavily upon the participation and contribution of its members, every person is important to team life and outcomes. And since each member brings a network of connections and commitments that define their personal journey, what team members care about is significant to the team. Good teams care about what their members care about. They care about family health and relationships. They care about commitments, groups, church involvement, and volunteer engagements. One of the reasons our mountaineering group is still roped together after thirty years is that we care about the passions and concerns of one another. We rope up to climb a mountain, but the rope is much stronger than that. The team relationships represented by the mountaineering rope connect us in life. We care about each other, the life journey that each of us is on. The team will be there on the rope if needed as each of us ascends summits and negotiates the valleys of life. Teams form for a purpose; they share something beyond themselves. They also share life, and strong team relationships assist us on our journey. In many ways the team is base camp for each person's climb through life.

Questions for reflection

- What teams or communities are important to your journey?

- What support system is required for each of your team memberships?

- What passions shape the members of your team? What fears eat away at them?

- To what larger expedition does your team contribute?

- Where is your base camp?

- How supportive is your family?

- How much investment do you make in your family? How much face-to-face time do you have with them? What passions drive them? What fears shape them?

- Is your family a rope team?

Chapter 10

Trails and summits

Teams share something beyond themselves

The Black Tusk

Jutting into the air like a rhinoceros horn, the Black Tusk captures the eye on a drive between Vancouver and Whistler. The ugly rock formation sits high and alone on a ridge above Lake Garibaldi, pointing defiantly at the sky. Don and I decided that this would be a nice one-day hike and climb. We studied the map and chose the trail from Rubble Creek to Lake Garibaldi, then up the ridge to the base of the Black Tusk. From there it would be a class three rock climb to the summit of the Tusk with views of Whistler Mountain, Blackcomb, and the beautiful North Vancouver mountains.

It was a sunny day and we started early knowing that we were tackling a 16-mile round trip with continuous elevation gain. I had been on the trail to Lake Garibaldi before and knew it was a steady 5.5-mile hike to the lake, with another 2.5 miles to the Tusk. I had taken various friends on the Lake Garibaldi hike in the past, and all of them had the same response. The hike was rigorously uphill all the way, but the lake snuggled in a cirque with a glacier backdrop was an emerald jewel. No one regretted visiting the lake, but many of my friends chose not to repeat the hike. Don and I started strong and enjoyed the steep ascent to the lake even though the pace we set could be felt in our legs. From Lake Garibaldi we hiked through wonderful fields of heather – brilliant red with fall color – and arrived at the Tusk well before lunch ready to climb the rock formation.

Our first surprise came when we saw the number of young people lined up at the base of the Tusk preparing to climb to its summit. Where had they come from? We had maintained a fast pace. No one had passed us and we passed very few persons on the hike from Rubble Creek. We waited in line for an opening and then scrambled up the rock to the summit only to find a large youth group sitting there eating lunch. Again we were surprised. How did they get here? The mystery was solved with our final surprise. When we stood on the summit and looked down the other side we saw a parking lot filled with cars at the end of a dirt road to a nearby powerline pole. The youth group had driven to the lot and walked about a quarter mile to the Tusk filled with relaxed energy as they climbed the rock. Don and I felt like two tired old men having walked a strenuous eight miles to get to this climb. We had to smile as we sat there eating our lunch listening to the babble of young conversation, knowing that they could see the cars waiting to take them home while we had another eight miles to walk downhill before we could even see our car. Two trails, one summit: Did we take the wrong one?

Choosing a trail

What trails do we follow? How do we choose a trail? These questions, of course, flow out of a prior question: *Are trails the way to summits or are summits objectives along the trail?* Which has priority, the trail or the summit? If Don and I had realized that we could drive to the base of the Black Tusk, would we have chosen the shorter trail? The answer is clearly No. The youth chattering on top of the Black Tusk had not experienced the cascading power of Rubble Creek, the peaceful ponds along the trail, the breathtaking majesty of Lake Garibaldi framed by its glaciers, the color of heather against the snow and sky, and the big eyed deer watching cautiously as we passed. They missed the physical exertion of a long steep trail, and the sense of wellbeing that follows a long, hard trip. They reached the summit but they missed the wilderness.

The trail we choose defines the parameters of our journey. There may or may not be a summit to climb on the trail, but the trail determines how steeply we will climb, how fast we can travel, the wilderness we can explore, the vistas we will see, the equipment we must carry, and the skills we should have. The journey begins with the trail. Journeys never end; they keep going as long as life keeps going. We can travel either direction on a trail and branch off in various directions. Summits have a defined objective. When we reach them we have completed the assignment. But the trail continues down from the summit and home again. Trails are about purpose, direction, and meaning. They take us beyond ourselves into the larger mission of life and relationships. Trails don't end when we have achieved our objective, reached the summit of the mountain before us. The trail continues.

Our rope team started thirty years ago on a trail from Crystal Lake over the Angeles Crest of the San Gabriel Mountains to Little Jimmy Campground. That trail launched our journey together, taught us how much we did not know, initiated lifelong relationships, and began to shape our understanding of how teams work together. The team shares something beyond itself – the vision and values around which it formed, the trail we choose to take together. And the trail continues; along the way we climb some mountains. It is the journey that matters, not how high or how far we can go.

This was a piece of wisdom I learned again from the Sherpas who guided our trek to Kala Pattar above the Mt. Everest Base Camp.[123] From the first day of the trek, the Sherpas told us not to focus on the summit of Kala Pattar or base camp as the measure of success. And consistently the Sherpas refused to talk about distance. Never would any guide refer to miles or kilometers. It was always days. Partly this is due to the impact that altitude and elevation gain have in measuring distance. It takes ten days to walk from Lukla to Lobuche. But it takes four days to walk from Lobuche to Lukla. And partly they did not focus on distance because they were not measuring by destination. They focused on one day at a time. They encouraged us to come for the trek not the summit. The summit of Kala Pattar above the Everest Base Camp is only one point on the trek – and not everyone should expect to go there. If the destination becomes the measure of success, many factors – health, weather, altitude – could make the trek a failure. If the trek *is* the destination, the trip will be a success regardless of how far we go.

I knew this advice. I know it as someone who has been turned back from several mountain summits because of weather or health or skill. And basically I have lived most of my life with this philosophy. I really do believe that life is about living – not accomplishments! But on this trip I was not listening. I had flown half way around the world to participate in this trek. However, I came for the wrong reason. I wanted to go to the Khumbu basin, to climb higher than 18,000 feet and look down on the Everest Base Camp. And I figured that I might not have such an opportunity again. So I focused strongly on the destination and channeled my energy each day to eating, drinking, sleeping, and staying healthy enough for the next day's trek. Without even realizing it, I followed the trail past incredibly beautiful sights focused on staying healthy enough for tomorrow. At 14,000 feet we were snowed in for three days and faced the high probability that we might not be able to go higher because of deep snow and no visibility. If you read my journal for those nights you can see me trying to justify why the trip was a success, even if we turned around there. It's not very convincing.

When I look at my pictures now, I am surprised how beautiful it was where we were snowed in at Dingboche. Yet in my journal I am complaining about the snow, the altitude, and the pungent smell of burning yak dung.

I would like to say that God met me at 14,000 feet, that I recognized the error of my ways, saw the beauty of the past two weeks, and went on not needing to reach the summit. Unfortunately that's not what happened. I had a very difficult time keeping perspective on this trek and I did not let go of the summit until I had reached it. Only on the way down did I begin to realize that this was an incredibly beautiful trail we were walking through remarkable villages and wonderful people. Only on the way down did I stop worrying about my health and strength and find time to reflect on what was happening … And then I got depressed. Then I realized that this goal that I have had for years – this trek to the Everest Base Camp – was behind me … It was over. The adventure of my life was done. That is a depressing thought!

It took me several days back home before I regained perspective and realized what I had done. I had focused on a destination – a summit – at the expense of the journey. And, like all destinations, when I got there I found it was only one more point on the trail, not the end. My need to reach the summit, teamed with my uncertainty about my ability to make it, focused all of my energy on the summit. I almost missed the wonders of the trail. Perhaps that is why I decided to walk the Wonderland Trail around Mt. Rainier this past fall. I wanted to immerse myself in the trail without a summit to distract me.

Summits have purpose, but trails give daily context to the journey. Choosing a trail is a statement of faith, a declaration of vision, mission, and hope. It is embracing a guiding purpose beyond ourselves. The trails we choose determine where we are going and who we want to be. Trails have as much to do with the way we travel together, the experiences we share as they do with the summits we climb – the objectives we achieve – along the journey.

Why do we choose a particular trail? Everyone responds to that question daily as we decide how to live our lives. And teams choose their trails with the same mix of motivations. Some trails like the route past Lake Garibaldi or the loop around Mt. Rainier are chosen for their beauty. Aesthetics takes precedence over convenience. Some trails are chosen because they are the easiest paths to take – that is why the trails were blazed in the first place.[124] Sometimes we choose trails appropriate to a particular rope team. Next week we will ski into the Sierras for a long weekend. If Newt is able to join us as we hope, we will choose a trail suitable for a seventy-three-year-old skier. Occasionally a trail is chosen because we follow a mentor – one who has gone on before and chosen a path that we want to follow. As we plan the thirtieth anniversary trip of our mountaineering team, we want to retrace the footsteps of John Muir along the John Muir Trail from Mt. Whitney to Yosemite Valley.

And always the trails are chosen with the purpose in mind. What do we want to accomplish? Where are we going? Why are we together as a team? The reason we form a team limits the trails that we choose. Even then we usually have choice. When we plan a trip into the Cottonwood Lakes Basin, our purposes are to spend the weekend together, enjoy the wilderness, and climb to the Pacific Crest. We can walk the Forest Service trail to Cottonwood Lakes camps or trek cross-country to a meadow we know completely isolated from other campers. We can climb Cirque Peak or Mt. Langley. We can approach Cirque Peak up the north side of its east ridge or on the north ridge from New Army Pass. Alternative trails spread out before us as we ponder the purpose of our journey. Together the team chooses the trail and the objectives by which it will measure its progress. The team envisions the trail it will take and identifies the summits it will climb along the way. The summits are exciting objectives but they are not the purpose, not the vision. The vision is about the trail to be walked. It includes reaching the summit and continuing back down to follow the trail and climb another summit. It is the trail that matters and how we walk it not the summits we climb or how high we can go.

The seduction of summits

George Mallory is famous for his response to the question: Why do you want to climb Mt. Everest? He replied: "Because it is there."[125] George Mallory participated in the third attempt to climb Mt. Everest in 1924. He disappeared on the mountain and his body was not found until 1999, seventy-five years later, with no indication whether he died in the ascent or on the way down from the summit. Why do we climb mountains? Because they are there. They loom large on the horizon and beckon us to try. They offer vista and scope, challenge and accomplishment. Mountain summits are seductive.

Our first serious summit attempt was included in the Sierra Club's Basic Mountaineering Training Course. We climbed 12,945-feet-high Mt. Banner in the Ritter Range of the Sierras. This was our training with rope, ice axe, and crampons climbing a glacier and class three rock to a significant summit. Standing on top we were exhilarated as we scanned the Sierra crest 360 degrees around us. Then to the south we saw Mt. Ritter, 200 feet higher – the big sister of the Ritter range – and we felt the challenge flow through our bodies. Further south we saw Mt. Whitney: at 14,494 feet, the tallest mountain in the 48 states. Though not a technical climb, the elevation lured us like a siren song and we began to plan.

That summer Newt, Larry Ferguson, and I climbed Mt. Whitney. It was the first of several trips members of our team have made to the summit of Mt. Whitney. It was our first taste of altitude and the headaches that accompany it and our first attempt to plan a strenuous trip on our own. I remember well our arguments about food. To cut down on weight it was suggested that we limit our food supply to instant breakfast. I objected. I was a young man who needed large quantities of food to fuel my hiking. Instant breakfast would not do it. We compromised with a reasonable menu of lightweight food but the highlight was the chicken we ate on top of Mt. Whitney. Larry's wife cooked chicken breasts Filipino-style, preserved to last without refrigeration. We basked in the sunshine on top of the mountain eating in style and reinforcing the pull of summits on our journey. Our thoughts turned to Mt. Ritter.

Mt. Ritter has eluded us to date. Three times we have tried to reach the summit. The first time weather stopped us at the base. The second time one short-term team member brought faulty equipment. His crampons would not work properly and he didn't have the patience to solve the problem. The third time we nearly reached the summit when the storm came in that resulted in Newt's serious fall. Three times we turned back, but the summit still calls. Even Newt still talks about trying it again. That summit is important to us but returning to climb again has been a higher priority. So Mt. Ritter still looms on our horizon and we will climb it one day.

In the meantime the volcanoes of Washington caught our attention: Mt. Baker, Mt. Rainier, Mt. Adams, Mt. St. Helens – each standing in splendid isolation along the Cascade Crest of the state. The solitary aloneness of these volcanoes probably enhances their allure. We set out to climb them all, but we have not yet succeeded. Brent and I climbed Mt. Baker one rainy weekend with a rope team from Canada. Nine of us climbed Mt. Rainer twenty-five years ago with a challenging traverse of the mountain. Brent and an occasional member of our team, Brian Van Dragt, climbed Mt. St. Helens after it erupted to look down into its amazing crater. Mt. Adams is still on our horizon since the powerful windstorm ended our single attempt to reach that summit.

Summits are seductive. They lure us to the top as though that were the end that we seek. When we reach the top we will have arrived. That is only temporarily true. Everyone who climbs mountains understands false summits. A false summit is the one you struggle to reach only to realize that the trail continues to a yet higher point marking the true summit of the mountain. On the trail of life, most summits are false summits. They are not the end we seek. They are only high points on a trail that continues. When the summit becomes the purpose, depression follows because the summit satisfies only temporarily. We always want more. Summits are important milestones along the trail, but the trail does not end at the top.

Summits do have an important role, however. They provide specific, visible, measurable objectives. They focus energy and assess progress. Reaching a summit achieves one objective on the trail, it demonstrates progress and it maintains momentum toward the purpose before us.[126] This is important for all of life, but essential for the life of a team. The team needs to set objectives and monitor its progress to reinforce its performance and growth.[127] Summits capture our imagination in a way that trails do not. They stand out as accomplishments when compared to walking for miles in the forest. They keep us motivated and they mark progress. They form the strategies that keep us moving forward. But summits do not replace purpose. Strategy should not replace mission, though that is frequently a temptation for teams and for organizations. The trail the team chooses will determine which summits it will climb, which objectives will achieve its purpose.

When I was on the trek to the Everest Base Camp we would ask our Sherpa guides what the trail was like ahead of us. They would laugh, hold up one hand with fingers splayed and using their other hand they would trace the fingers and spaces between, commenting: "The trail ahead is like every Himalayan trail – up and down, up and down, up and down." The trail defines our journey. Summits and valleys measure progress along the way.

Managing adversity

When storms hit we turn back. That has been a principle of our rope team from the beginning. We want to reach the summit, but we know the trail lasts a lifetime and we want to live to climb again. Too many climbers have died because they needed to reach the summit. It is hard to turn back when we are close to the top. This is especially true when the summit objective has replaced the purpose of the trail. If the summit looms too large in our vision, the choice to turn back is difficult. If the trail is kept before us – the larger picture of our shared vision – turning back is only a temporary adjustment in strategy. The team has a responsibility to keep its shared vision alive and to ensure that the long-range vision defines its short-term decisions.

I think there is a difference between turning back from a summit attempt and turning back from a trail. Trails have no end; they go both directions. Trails are about continuing to walk toward a desired future. We do not go back; we only experience part of the trail anew. To stop walking on the trail would be to give up, to lose sight of the mission, the purpose, even of life. Summits on the other hand are limited objectives, specific strategies. We turn back from summits for a variety of reasons to try again later or to choose a different summit to climb. A team turns away from a strategy more easily than it changes its purpose. It is the shared vision of purpose that shapes strategic decisions.

Why do we turn back from a summit? Storms are the most frequent reason. When any person on the team believes it is unsafe to continue, we turn back. When a storm arrives and conditions begin to deteriorate, the designated leader turns us back automatically because that's one of our agreed-upon policies. When the objective is unreasonable or the cost is too high, we turn back. On the trek around Mt. Rainier we encountered a bridge over the Paradise River partially washed out by flooding from the previous night's storm. If our life depended upon crossing that river we might have been able to do it, even though much of it was underwater, but we did have other options and the risk was greater than we deemed necessary so we backtracked three miles to a secure crossing and continued from there. We finished the complete trail, but we changed our strategies as needed. The cost of a strategy may turn us away. Lene Gammelgaard, one of the climbers on the fateful 1996 Everest climb, put it bluntly: "Mount Everest taught me a valuable lesson. I will never again expose myself to that amount of objective risk. Never! Being alive is precious. Life is so short."[128] When we lack the skill or equipment we turn back. Faulty equipment ended one of our attempts at Mt. Ritter. On one of our climbs of Temple Crag in the Palisades Range we chose a route that brought us to a final pitch that we didn't have the skills to negotiate. We turned back and later climbed it on a route we were competent to attempt. And we turn back when we run out of time. If we cannot reach the summit or destination and back within our predetermined timeframe, we make the decision to turn around at the specified time and rethink the plan for a future trip. This was the primary contributor to the 1996 Everest disaster. The lure of the summit caused climbers who knew better to violate their own failsafe timeframes and continue toward the summit when they should have turned around. That decision alone cost the lives of several climbers, including two of the team leaders.

Every team faces obstacles, barriers to completion of a targeted objective. The threat raised by any particular obstacle depends as much on the team's preparation and competence as it does on the obstacle itself.[129] When the vision is clear, the policies understood and the decision-making process accepted, the team is capable of exercising its wisdom and managing the problem. Sometimes the team will decide to turn back and rethink that strategy. Sometimes it will find a way around the obstacle, continuing forward. Sometimes a different strategy will be employed. The team is responsible to keep the larger vision in focus and make accountable judgments about its summit objectives in light of its shared purpose. When a team is not prepared or focuses excessively on the objective at hand rather than the mission that defines it, turning back can be demoralizing, draining enthusiasm and damaging team relationships. However, the team shares something beyond itself – a shared vision that defines its purpose and identity. The team, often through its designated leader, must keep that vision in focus to manage the adversity that occurs naturally along the trail it walks together.

Good teams do not shy away from the decision to turn back from a summit objective. They make the decision together. But a good team, I believe, will never allow its members to turn away from the trail, to turn their backs on the journey. We are roped together as a team. Together we decide to ascend a summit or turn back. Together we choose a purpose and follow a trail. To untie from the rope is a choice to separate from the team. We travel the trail together. When Chris Bonnington led the British climb of Everest in 1975, Doug Scott and Dougal Haston were the first rope team to reach the summit. Immediately behind them came Mick Burke and Martin Boysten. The second rope team was nearly at the summit when Boysten's oxygen failed. He had to return to camp. Mick Burke, so close to his personal objective, untied from the climbing rope and headed toward the summit alone. He died in that attempt.[130] The team stays on the trail, keeps its purpose before it, faces problems, manages adversity, decides together about summits, and remains a team. The rope makes the team visible. The team chooses the trail it follows.

The trail is not wilderness

"A trail by definition is not wilderness even though it be a corridor of civilization barely a foot wide."[131] I have been using trail as a metaphor for direction, purpose, and meaning for a team roped together by relationships. However, a trail suggests that others have gone before. Often we start down paths blazed by someone else, building on what they have learned. In the wilderness, when a new path is chosen that others should follow, we mark the trail with ducks and cairns – small rocks on larger ones, or small piles of rocks. These benchmarks indicate the route that was taken, making it easier for those following. As more and more people choose to follow a particular trail it gains permanence, first from accumulated footprints, then from the work of individuals and organizations establishing a route through the wilderness. The trail reveals that someone has been here before and thinks this is the best way forward. It is a foundation for learning upon which we can build. The purpose of a team may be to do well what others have pioneered. In such cases, the team stays on the trail, reinforcing it for those who will follow and protecting it from erosion. Trails, purposes, visions, and passions need to be cared for and nurtured. Too many distractions, wanderings from the path break down the integrity of the trail and leave it vulnerable to weather and erosion. Consequently, established trail systems come with signage asking us to "Stay on the Trail" – not to cut switchbacks and take shortcuts that undermine the stability of the trail. I think this analogy holds for the work we do in teams as well, staying focused on the purpose, stewarding resources, and doing things right.

All trails exist, however, because someone first ventured into the wilderness. At one time it was unmarked, wild country until someone found a way through and marked it for others to follow. Frequently, teams will choose a direction of travel that causes them to leave the established trail and venture into the wilderness. Early explorers did this to search for new routes, passages through mountains, fords across rivers, new country to claim. More often today we head into the wilderness to seek solitude, a quiet place away from the press of civilization, a place to reflect on the Creation around us. Trekking cross-country with a map and compass requires more skill than following the trail others have walked, but it opens new vistas and discovers new possibilities. When we visit the Cottonwood Lakes basin, we start on the established trail but after a few miles we branch off using map, compass, and geography to locate a beautiful meadow fed by a clear mountain stream teaming with Golden Trout. There is no trail to this meadow, even though now we know exactly where it is located on a topographical map. To preserve the solitude of this place and the wilderness surrounding it we try not to take the same route every time we visit. We are not trying to leave a trail. We want to preserve the solitude of wilderness. The meadow is there for others to discover as well. But even the footprints we leave behind can be followed, for better or worse. When we chose a route up Mt. Rainier, we followed no trail except for one critical portion where we needed to find a safe way through. There we found footprints and followed them through the crevasses only to discover that we were trailing behind a herd of mountain goats! Fortunately they knew the route better than we did. Yet nine of us in a row climbing through glacier and snow left a discernible trail behind us that others did follow as they attempted to reach the summit from that side of the mountain. Trails civilize wilderness for those who follow. Sometimes that is good; sometimes it is a loss. Teams usually follow trails laid down by those who have gone before. Often they branch off, exploring new territory, leaving a trail for others to follow. Sometimes, however, the trail does not lead anywhere that we want to go and is not worth following.

Measuring progress

So where are we going? That of course is the defining question for every team. What is the mission that brings us together? What do we want to accomplish together? Who do we want to be together? Trails and summits are about sharing something larger than ourselves, something beyond the team – a vision of what could be, a vision of who we want to be. The defining mission, vision, or purpose that forms the team is the standard against which progress must be continually measured. And measurement is important. We tend to accomplish that which we measure. We keep track of what we think is important. Teams need to clarify what they want to accomplish together, measure their progress and adapt their strategies to that feedback. This is a team project. Teams do not respond well to outside standards. The team needs to design, embrace, and hold itself accountable to its own expectations and outcomes.[132]

Teams succeed because they choose to walk a portion of the trail together. Together they choose the trail and define the results that they seek. They choose together which summits to climb and together they celebrate their achievements. The team learns from experience and failure and keeps moving on their chosen trail. They keep one eye on the horizon – where they are going – and one eye on the trail – where they choose to place the next foot. They decide when to climb over a summit and when to walk around a mountain. These are team decisions as they measure the team's progress along the trail. They are decisions made by the team because the team is roped together. Everyone has a vested interest in answering the questions. Teams measure distance, elevation, summits, objectives, health, supplies, and participation of members. Reaching the summit is one measure of progress. Where we are on the trail is a measure of maturity. Both contribute to the legacy found in the footprints the team leaves behind.

Questions for reflection

- What is the purpose of your journey?

- How would your team describe the trail you have chosen in terms of a shared vision and shared values?

- What summit dominates your horizon?

- What summits are the key objectives for the next year?

- What might turn you back from your objective?

- Under what conditions would you abandon the trail – the mission or purpose that brings the team together?

- How are you marking your trail in a way that others can follow and learn from your accomplishment?

- Where will those following your footprints today find themselves tomorrow?

- How do you measure progress on the trail you have chosen?

- Where are you going?

Conclusion: On the summit

Team success is measured by legacy

The rope team

This year our mountaineering group will celebrate its thirtieth anniversary as a rope team. Whether we will complete the John Muir Trail is still a matter of discussion, but at some point on this anniversary trip we will cross a summit or high pass in the Sierra Nevada Mountains of California and pause to reflect on three decades of life roped together. From this summit perspective we will consider the mountains we have climbed, the backcountry in which we've skied, and the rivers we have canoed. We will envision the wilderness we explored from British Columbia to California, from the Pacific Ocean to the Rocky Mountains. We will think about the miles covered, the nights spent in the mountains, the risks we took, and the laughs we've had. We will celebrate what we have accomplished as a team of men climbing mountains. But we will also give thanks for the impact this team has had on our lives.

We accomplished together far more than any one of us would have imagined when we took our first trip together in 1975. With the pull of the rope we were encouraged to sharpen our skills, upgrade our equipment, and attempt adventures we might otherwise have missed. Over the past thirty years every one of us has become more proficient in wilderness survival then we ever would have achieved on our own. The team together has climbed mountains that few would attempt alone.

However, we also are aware of the strength we have all drawn from this rope team to walk the longer trail of life, to climb the summits of career, to negotiate the rapids of relational passages with parents, spouses, and children. Everyone's journey includes the mountain highs of success and the valleys of failure and depression. Sorrow and joy cross everyone's path. The rope team has provided a powerful base camp, committed caring relationships where we find encouragement, perspective, and help when it is needed. A community where we belong, where who we are and what we can contribute are valued, where we are encouraged to risk learning and growth in the pursuit of our common vision is a wonderful foundation from which to foray into the adventures of life. We have been better parents, husbands, and neighbors because we roped up to climb mountains with friends.

And I believe we have become more capable leaders. Our experience on the rope has encouraged us to develop teams in the organizations where we exercise leadership. When we think about teams in our various organizational settings, we talk about teamwork, organizations as expeditions, roping up together, and leading teams.

Teamwork

Teamwork is a strategy – a way of working together to accomplish something that we believe is worth doing. Being a team is not the purpose of an organization, nor does it alone provide meaning for a life. It is not the trail we walk; it is one way to walk on the trail. Teams exist to pursue mission, to achieve a purpose. They focus resources and energy on chosen results. And they build on the relational nature of life and draw on the social connections that define us as human beings as we work together toward a common goal. Because teamwork is a tapestry of results *and* relationships, teams are an effective strategy for companies and organizations to encourage. They serve the chosen purpose that gives meaning to our lives while nurturing the community relationships in which we find identity and fulfillment. Teams take seriously the rope that connects members, understanding that strong relationships support shared purpose and increase effectiveness. Good teams, by definition, recognize that they are roped up and work to keep the rope strong. Strong ropes encourage team members' growth and further team accomplishments. The legacy of a team therefore will be seen in the potential released in its members as well as the results accomplished by its efforts.

Organization as expedition

A team approach to leadership suggests that organizations see themselves as expeditions – focused networks of people providing resources, knowledge, information, technical expertise, labor, and organization for a trek down a particular trail, with specific summits to climb. The expedition is intensely sighted on its objective, its mission. It exists for a reason. It does not exist just to stay in business. The expedition is established to enable its rope teams to reach the expedition goals. All of the expedition resources are directed toward putting strong teams in place for the accomplishment of objectives. The expedition sets the direction, gathers the resources, and allocates them strategically in support of the climbing teams. Leadership is selected to facilitate these expedition responsibilities, always recognizing the importance of maintaining healthy, focused rope teams. And because rope teams will be responsible for ultimate achievement of objectives, the expedition allows teams to contribute to corporate decisions without abdicating the authority given to the expedition leaders.

Roping up together

The rope team is the basic unit of an expedition and the model captures our vision of an effective working team. On the journey through this book we have seen that:

Teams are formed by interdependent relationships. Leaders and followers are roped together. Their successes and failures are linked as they move toward the objective together. What happens to one happens to all.

Teams manage diversity within clearly defined community. Diversity enriches capacity for a team but only within the limits of its common culture. Compatibility, stability and shared values define the relationships at the heart of the community. Building, nurturing, and protecting those relationships is essential to the effectiveness of a team.

Teams share responsibility and mutual accountability based on trust. Teams depend on this. Team members are responsible for themselves and accountable to the team for their contribution to its mission. There is also mutual responsibility and accountability for the team among team members reinforced by honest communication and open trust.

Teams require shared leadership. Leadership is one of many responsibilities delegated by the team. Leadership is a relationship of influence serving the team purpose and its members. However, decisions are made by the team and conflict is managed by the team because in the end the team is the leader.

Teams create a safe environment for development. Once again the rope provides a powerful image as team members belay one another to encourage the risk of learning and growth. Trusting relationships embrace vulnerability, forgive failure, and mentor the development of team members.

Teams build community. Teams are relational communities; this is what sets them apart from work groups. They accomplish their mission by creating a place where members belong, where their contribution is valued and they are encouraged to grow.

Team memory creates and reinforces culture. Memory lays the foundations for building the team and feeds the soul of the community. It learns from the past, rekindles relational intimacy and encourages growth.

Teams allow humor to keep things in perspective. Humor creates just the right amount of slack in the rope. It vents emotions and lowers masks and allows the team to work seriously together as fallible, striving human beings.

Teams embrace the whole person and family. Teams are only as strong as the members, each of whom represents a personal mix of family, friends, passions, and fears. Rope teams rely upon personal base camps to support their commitment to climb.

Teams share something beyond themselves. Teams are formed for a purpose. A trail is chosen which sets the direction and defines the team. Summits loom large as objectives to be reached. The energy generated by the relationships of community is always focused on the trail ahead, the summit being climbed. It is that shared vision that calls the team together and becomes the measure of its success.

Leading teams

As the vision is shared, leadership on teams is shared. Everyone on the rope leads and follows. Every member owns the outcomes and seeks to influence results. Leadership is distributed. On effective teams, that will be true whether or not the leader is appointed by the organization. *Teams are roped up leaders.* But as noted above, effective teams delegate specific responsibilities to one of the members to serve them as leader. Building on an outline suggested by Jon Katzenbach and Douglas Smith[133] I think leaders of teams:

- Keep the purpose and goals before the team always and make sure they are shared by all members and perceived as meaningful.
- Build commitment and confidence within and among members, making sure that everyone is tied into the rope and belayed.
- Strengthen the mix of technical and relational skills. Make sure everyone understands the skills needed and keeps honing their abilities. Encourage the continual social interactions that build community.
- Manage outside relationships with the larger organization or expedition and secure the support services required by the team.
- Create opportunities for others to lead by delegating leadership back to team members for specific areas of responsibility.
- Do real work. The leader is one member of the team roped up like everyone else – not "the leader," but one member with leadership responsibility for this particular objective.

Basically, team members in the office or on the rope are all treated like leaders; they are expected to own results. They are invited to influence outcomes and followed when they lead. They are valued as persons and trusted for the integrity of their character. Strong members make strong teams, and effective teams continue to strengthen their members. And roped together, dependent on each other, the team climbs to the summit and looks for the next mountain to climb.

The trail continues

When our rope team pauses to reflect on the past thirty years, I am sure that this mountain top reminiscing will be a time of joyful celebration and freeing laughter as we recount our years together. However, this is only a summit. The trail continues. We will shoulder our packs, start down the other side and begin the fourth decade of climbing together. We are a rope team – a community of relationships – with mountains to climb hovering on the horizon.

Notes

[1] Jean Lipman-Blumen and Harold J. Leavitt, *Hot Groups: Seeding Them, Feeding Them, and Using Them to Ignite Your Organization* (Oxford: Oxford University Press, 1999), 21.

[2] With apologies to and permission from Don Dwyer, I will use Don in reference to Don Bosch and Dwyer in reference to Don Dwyer to facilitate reading.

[3] Stephen Garber, *The Fabric of Faithfulness* (Downers Grove: IVP, 1994), 171.

[4] Richard J. Leider and David A. Shapiro, *Claiming Your Place at the Fire: Living the Second Half of your Life on Purpose* (San Francisco: Berrett-Koehler, 2004), vii.

[5] Joe Simpson, *Touching the Void* (New York: HarperCollins, 1989).

[6] Simpson, *Touching the Void* (quote taken from documentary movie script).

[7] Several months later I met a man whose rope team had attempted the same climb of Mt. Rainier two days after our trip. They of course had the good fortune to follow our footprints for most of the way. However, when they reached the knife-edge they took one look and decided it was impassable and followed the now well-entrenched footprints back down to the car.

[8] Jon R. Katzenbach and Douglas K. Smith, *The Wisdom of Teams: Creating the High-Performance Organization* (New York: HarperCollins, 1993, 1999), 45.

[9] Margarita Mayo, James R. Meindl, and Juan-Carlos Pastor, "Shared Leadership in Work Teams," in *Shared Leadership: Reframing the Hows and Whys of Leadership*, ed. Craig L.

Pearce and Jay A. Conger (Thousand Oaks: Sage Publications, 2003), 195.

[10] Lipman-Blumen and Leavitt, *Hot Groups*, 3.

[11] Paul Hersey and Kenneth H. Blanchard, *Management of Organizational Behavior* (Englewood Cliffs: Prentice Hall, 1988), 5.

[12] John Roskelly, *Nanda Devi* (Harrisburg: Stackpole Books, 1987).

[13] Hersey and Blanchard, *Management of Organizational Behavior*, 171.

[14] James M. Kouzes and Barry Z. Posner, *The Leadership Challenge*. 3rd ed. (San Francisco: Jossey-Bass, 2002), 248.

[15] Lee Ellis, *Leading Talents, Leading Teams: Aligning People, Passions, and Positions for Maximum Performance* (Chicago: Northfield Publishing, 2003), 183.

[16] J. Richard Hackman, *Leading Teams: Setting the Stage for Great Performances* (Boston: Harvard Business School Press, 2002), 23.

[17] Lipman-Blumen and Leavitt, *Hot Groups*, 25–26.

[18] Michael Useem, Jerry Useem, and Paul Asel, *Upward Bound* (New York: Crown Business, 2003), 9.

[19] Hackman, *Leading Teams*, 122–123.

[20] Hackman, *Leading Teams*, 56.

[21] Max De Pree, *Leadership is an Art* (East Lansing: Michigan State University Press, 1987), xvi.

[22] Hackman, *Leading Teams*, 88.

[23] Hackman, *Leading Teams*, 119.

[24] Lipman-Blumen and Leavitt, *Hot Groups*, 155.

[25] Katzenbach and Smith, *The Wisdom of Teams*, 45.

[26] Ken Blanchard, *Inside Guide*, February 1991, 12.

[27] Ellis, *Leading Talents, Leading Teams*, 169.

[28] Ellis, *Leading Talents, Leading Teams*, 156.

[29] Hackman, *Leading Teams*, 56.

[30] Edgar H. Schein, *Organizational Culture and Leadership*, 2nd ed. (San Francisco: Jossey-Bass, 1992), 15.

[31] Hackman, *Leading Teams*, 66.

[32] Daniel Goleman, "What makes a Leader?" *Harvard Business Review* (November–December, 1998), 94.

[33] Ellis, *Leading Talents, Leading Teams*, 228.

34 Robert E. Kelley, *How to be a Star at Work* (New York: Random House, 1999), 204.

35 Daniel Goleman, *Working with Emotional Intelligence* (New York: Bantam Books, 1998), 208–211.

36 Daniel Goleman, Richard Boyatzis, and Annie McKee, *Primal Leadership* (Boston: Harvard Business School Press, 2002), 181.

37 Katzenbach and Smith, *The Wisdom of Teams*, 15.

38 Glenn M. Parker, *Team Players and Teamwork: The New Competitive Business Strategy* (San Francisco: Jossey-Bass, 1990), 77.

39 Hackman, *Leading Teams*, 15.

40 Chris Bonington, *Everest the Hard Way* (New York: Hodder & Stoughton, 1976).

41 Michael Useem, *The Leadership Moment* (New York: Random House, 1998), 94–126.

42 Katzenbach and Smith, *The Wisdom of Teams*, 60.

43 William Golding, *The Lord of the Flies* (New York: Perigee, 1954), 33.

44 The Mountaineers, a wilderness organization in Seattle, years ago distributed a list of the ten essential items "everyone who ventures onto a trail or into the backcountry should have:" 1. Navigation (map and compass), 2. Sun protection, 3. Insulation (extra clothing), 4. Illumination (flashlight/headlamp), 5. First-aid supplies, 6. Fire, 7. Repair kit and tools, 8. Nutrition (extra food), 9. Hydration (extra water), 10. Emergency shelter. See www.mountaineers.org/.

45 Stacy Allison, "Peak Performers: Leading Teams in High Places," in Michael Useem, Jerry Useem, and Paul Asel, *Upward Bound* (New York: Crown Business, 2003), 52–54.

46 Gary A. Yukl, *Leadership in Organizations* (Englewood Cliffs: Prentice Hall, 1981), 3. See also Howard Gardner, *Leading Minds* (New York: Basic Books, 1996), 8–9.

47 Hersey and Blanchard, *Management of Organizational Behavior*, 5.

48 See Walter C. Wright, *Relational Leadership* (Carlisle: Paternoster, 2000), 29–44.

49 James M. Kouzes and Barry Z. Posner, *Credibility* (San Francisco: Jossey-Bass, 1993), 59.

[50] See Max De Pree, *Leadership Jazz* (New York: Doubleday, 1992), 1–3.

[51] De Pree, *Leadership is an Art*, 61.

[52] Katzenbach and Smith, *The Wisdom of Teams*, 132.

[53] Allison, "Peak Performers," 73.

[54] Mayo, Meindl, and Pastor, "Shared Leadership in Work Teams," 195.

[55] W. Warner Burke, "Leadership as Empowering Others," in *Executive Power*, ed. Suresh Srivastva (San Francisco: Jossey-Bass, 1986), 65.

[56] Katzenbach and Smith, *The Wisdom of Teams*, 132.

[57] C. Shawn Burke, Stephen M. Fiore, and Eduardo Salas, "The Role of Shared Cognition in Enabling Shared Leadership and Team Adaptability," in *Shared Leadership,* ed. Craig L. Pearce and Jay A. Conger (Thousand Oaks: Sage Publications, 2003), 105.

[58] Parker, *Team Players and Teamwork*, 44.

[59] Peggy Ferber, ed., *Mountaineering: The Freedom of the Hills,* 3rd ed. (Seattle: The Mountaineers, 1974), 125.

[60] Patrick Lencioni, *The Five Dysfunctions of a Team* (San Francisco: Jossey-Bass, 2002), 202.

[61] Richard Gorsuch, *Building Peace: The 3 Pillars Approach* (Unpublished manuscript, 2004).

[62] De Pree, *Leadership Jazz,* 153.

[63] Ferber, *Mountaineering*, 137.

[64] Ferber, *Mountaineering*, 125.

[65] Jim Collins, "Leadership Lessons of a Rock Climber," *Fast Company,* December 2003, 104.

[66] Kouzes and Posner, *The Leadership Challenge*, 244.

[67] Kouzes and Posner, *The Leadership Challenge*, 247.

[68] Joseph A. Maciariello, *Lasting Value* (New York: John Wiley & Sons, 2000), 208.

[69] Kouzes and Posner, *The Leadership Challenge,* 214.

[70] Mark Wellman and John Flinn, *Climbing Back* (Waco: WRS Publishing, 1992), 90–110.

[71] HighBeam Research, "Wellman Strikes Again," October 1, 1999. See also http://static.highbeam.com/p/paraplegianews/october011999.

72 See Walter C. Wright, *Mentoring: The Promise of Relational Leadership* (Bletchley: Paternoster Press, 2004).

73 Rodrigo Jordan, "Strategy at the Crux: Life-and-Death Choices on Everest and K2," in Michael Useem, Jerry Useem, and Paul Asel, *Upward Bound* (New York: Crown Business, 2003), 167.

74 Ferber, *Mountaineering*, 137.

75 Wright, *Relational Leadership*, 38.

76 Hackman, *Leading Teams*, 27.

77 Michael Ray, *The Highest Goal* (San Francisco: Jossey-Bass, 2004), 108.

78 Max De Pree, "Foreword," in Walter C. Wright, *Mentoring: The Promise of Relational Leadership* (Bletchley: Paternoster Press, 2004), xv.

79 Sherry B. Ortner, *Life and Death on Mt. Everest* (Princeton: Princeton University Press, 1999), 11.

80 Jean Lipman-Blumen, *The Allure of Toxic Leaders* (Oxford: Oxford University Press, 2005), 38.

81 Leider and Shapiro, *Claiming Your Place at the Fire*, 50.

82 Leider and Shapiro, *Claiming Your Place at the Fire*, 57.

83 Leider and Shapiro, *Claiming Your Place at the Fire*, ix–xv.

84 Warren Bennis, *On Becoming a Leader* (New York: Addison-Wesley Publishing, 1989), 114–115.

85 Kouzes and Posner, *The Leadership Challenge*, 143.

86 Peter Block, *The Answer to How Is Yes* (San Francisco: Berrett-Koehler Publishers, 2002).

87 Bill Jensen, *Simplicity* (Cambridge: Perseus Books, 2000), 93.

88 Kouzes and Posner, *The Leadership Challenge*, 118.

89 Kenneth Pargament, *The Psychology of Religion and Coping* (New York: Guilford Press, 1997), 100.

90 Goleman, Boyatzis, and McKee, *Primal Leadership*, 163.

91 Kouzes and Posner, *The Leadership Challenge*, 119–121.

92 Goleman, Boyatzis, and McKee, *Primal Leadership*, 14.

93 Parker, *Team Players and Teamwork*, 34–35.

94 Ronald P. Culberson, "Humor At Work" (The Art Gliner Center for Humor Studies, University of Maryland, 2004). See also www.amst.umd.edu/humorcenter/essays/culterson5.htm.

95 Mission Statement, The Art Gliner Center for Humor Studies, University of Maryland, 2004. See also http://amst.umd.edu/humorcenter/mission.html.

[96] Parker, *Team Players and Teamwork*, 35.

[97] University of Michigan, Human Resources and Affirmative Action: Building Great Places to Work Initiative (www.umich.edu/~hraa/greatplaces/camaraderie.html); Ronald P. Culberson, "Humor at Work: How to Add a Bolt of 'Lighten'ing to Your Career" (Art Gliner Center for Humor Studies, University of Maryland), (http:www.amst.umd.edu/humorcenter/ essays/culberson1.htm).

[98] Parker, *Team Players and Teamwork*, 36.

[99] Culberson, "Humor at Work."

[100] Bennis, *On Becoming a Leader*, 115.

[101] Mihaly Csikszentmihalyi, *Finding Flow: The Psychology of Engagement with Everyday Life* (New York: Basic Books, 1997), in Kouzes and Posner, *The Leadership Challenge*, 318.

[102] David Granirer, "Laughing Your Way to Organizational Health" (www.psychocomic.com/ART-0006.htm).

[103] A.J.S. Rayl, "Humor: A Mind-Body Connection," 14: 1, October 2, 2000.

[104] Michael D. Yapko, *Hand-Me-Down Blues* (New York: St. Martin's Press, 1999), 109.

[105] Kouzes and Posner, *The Leadership Challenge*, 198.

[106] Kelley, *How to be a Star at Work*, 210.

[107] Jon Krakauer, *Into Thin Air* (New York: Willard, 1997), Anatoli Boukreev and G. Weston DeWalt, *The Climb* (New York: St. Martin's Press, 1997), Lene Gammelgaard, *Climbing High* (Seattle: Seal Press, 1999), Sherry B. Ortner, *Life and Death on Mt. Everest* (Princeton: Princeton University Press, 1999), Beck Weathers with Stephen G. Michaud, *Left for Dead* (New York: Dell, 2001).

[108] Adventure Consultants Website, December 21, 2004 (http://www.adventureconsultants.co.nz/AdventureInternational/Everestsummitlist/).

[109] Krakauer, Jon, *Into Thin Air*, xv.

[110] Weathers, *Left for Dead*.

[111] Pargament, *The Psychology of Religion and Coping*, 85–86.

[112] Weathers, *Left for Dead*, 56–57.

[113] Weathers, *Left for Dead*, 336.

[114] Weathers, *Left for Dead*, 338.

[115] Ortner, *Life and Death on Mt. Everest*, 9–11.

[116] Weathers, *Left for Dead*, 36.

[117] Pargament, *The Psychology of Religion and Coping*, 90.

[118] Pargament, *The Psychology of Religion and Coping*, 42.

[119] De Pree, *Leadership is an Art*, 8.

[120] Warren G. Bennis and Robert J. Thomas, *Geeks and Geezers: How Era, Values and Defining Moments Shape Leaders* (Boston: Harvard Business School Press, 2002), 14.

[121] Goleman, Boyatzis, and McKee, *Primal Leadership*, 14.

[122] Sheldon Zedeck, ed., *Work, Families and Organizations* (San Francisco: Jossey-Bass, 1992), 7.

[123] This story was first told in Wright, *Mentoring*, xxiv–xxvi.

[124] Ferber, *Mountaineering*, 82.

[125] Ortner, *Life and Death on Mt. Everest*, 3.

[126] Jim Collins, *Good to Great* (New York: HarperBusiness, 2001), 174.

[127] Hackman, *Leading Teams*, 134.

[128] Gammelgaard, *Climbing High*, 206.

[129] Katzenbach and Smith, *The Wisdom of Teams*, 150.

[130] Bonington, *Everest the Hard Way*, 179–183.

[131] Ferber, *Mountaineering*, 81.

[132] Katzenbach and Smith, *The Wisdom of Teams*, 60.

[133] Katzenbach and Smith, *The Wisdom of Teams*, 139–144.